The Conqueror's Code

Saladin Principles for Life and Leadership

A.A. Castor

Table of Contents

The Conqueror's Code: Saladin Principles for Life and Leadership

A.A. Castor

A.A. Castor

Dedication

To my beloved family,

Your unconditional love, unwavering support, and endless encouragement have been my greatest blessings. From the earliest days of dreaming to the challenging moments of writing, you have stood by me with patience and belief. This book is as much yours as it is mine, a reflection of the values you've instilled and the faith you've shown in me. Thank you for being my rock and my inspiration.

To my dear friends,

Your friendship has illuminated my path with laughter, shared moments, and invaluable support. You've cheered me on through every triumph and lifted me up through every challenge. Your belief in my endeavors has been a source of strength and motivation. This book is a testament to the power of friendship, and I am grateful for each of you who has walked this journey by my side.

To God,

Your grace and guidance have been my constant companions. In moments of doubt, you've shown me the way; in moments of joy, you've multiplied my gratitude. This book is a testament to your faithfulness and the blessings you've bestowed upon me. May it serve as a reflection of your love and the lessons you continue to teach me.

With heartfelt gratitude and love,

A.A. Castor

Copyright © 2024 by A.A. Castor

Philippine Copyright Law:

Why I Am Writing This Book

As I reflect on the challenges we face in modern leadership—whether in business, community, or personal life—I find myself continually drawn to the lessons of the past. History offers us powerful examples of individuals whose actions, values, and character have left a lasting impact on the world. One of the most profound figures in this regard is Salah ad-Din Yusuf ibn Ayyub, a leader who, despite the turbulence of his time, demonstrated the qualities of compassion, integrity, and wisdom that we still admire today.

I am writing *The Conqueror's Code: Salah ad-Din's Principles for Life and Leadership* to bring the enduring lessons of this remarkable leader to a modern audience. Salah ad-Din's story is not just about military victories or political strategy; it is about the values that define true leadership—honor, humility, justice, and the pursuit of a higher purpose. In a world that often prioritizes short-term success and personal ambition, his example serves as a reminder that leadership is not just about power, but about how we treat others and the legacy we leave behind.

Through this book, my hope is to provide readers with practical insights that they can apply in their own lives—whether in their careers, relationships, or community work. By examining Salah ad-Din's life and leadership, I aim to inspire individuals to lead with integrity, make decisions with wisdom, and approach challenges with compassion.

I believe that we all have the potential to lead, not just in formal positions of power, but in our everyday actions. Whether we are managing a team, raising a family, or contributing to our communities, the principles that guided Salah ad-Din can help us become better, more effective, and more compassionate leaders. This book is my way of sharing these timeless lessons with you.

Warning and Disclaimer

The contents of *The Conqueror's Code: Salah ad-Din's Principles for Life and Leadership* are intended for educational and inspirational purposes only. The information, examples, and interpretations provided in this book reflect the author's personal research and views on the life and leadership of Salah ad-Din Yusuf ibn Ayyub. While every effort has been made to ensure the accuracy of historical events and the application of leadership principles, the reader is encouraged to conduct independent research and verify historical facts as appropriate.

This book is not intended to serve as professional advice in areas such as business management, legal matters, or personal development coaching. Readers should seek guidance from qualified professionals for specific advice regarding leadership, business decisions, or personal matters.

The author and publisher assume no responsibility or liability for any outcomes, actions, or decisions taken based on the information provided in this book. The lessons and principles discussed are meant to inspire thoughtful reflection and self-improvement, but results may vary based on individual circumstances and actions.

About the Author

A.A. Castor is an author and researcher deeply passionate about leadership, history, and philosophy. With a keen interest in exploring the lives of influential figures from various cultures and eras, Castor brings historical lessons into the modern world, demonstrating how timeless principles can be applied to contemporary leadership, personal growth, and success. His writing emphasizes values such as integrity, compassion, and wisdom, drawing on historical examples to inspire readers across a range of fields.

A.A. Castor has written extensively on topics including strategic leadership, cultural history, and the intersection of ethics and power. His works blend historical insight with practical application, helping modern readers understand how the past can inform their approach to challenges in their personal and professional lives.

Castor's latest work, *The Conqueror's Code: Salah ad-Din's Principles for Life and Leadership*, delves into the life of one of history's most revered leaders, examining how his values and actions continue to offer valuable lessons for modern readers. By exploring Salah ad-Din's legacy, Castor aims to inspire leaders, professionals, and individuals to lead with honor, wisdom, and compassion.

Introduction: The Sultan and His Legacy

Salah ad-Din's Rise to Power

Early Life and Background

Salah ad-Din Yusuf ibn Ayyub, widely known in the Western world as Saladin, was born in 1137 or 1138 in Tikrit, in present-day Iraq. He hailed from a Kurdish family with a lineage tracing back to the famed Imad ad-Din Zengi, a prominent Muslim leader of the time. Salah ad-Din's upbringing in a politically active family provided him with early exposure to the intricacies of leadership and governance. His father, Najm ad-Din Ayyub, served as a governor in various regions, including Baalbek, Tikrit, and Damascus, instilling in Salah ad-Din a deep understanding of both administrative duties and military strategy.

Education and Early Career

Salah ad-Din received a comprehensive education that combined religious studies with military training. This dual focus equipped him with the knowledge to lead both spiritually and militarily, a balance that would define his later rule. Demonstrating exceptional prowess from a young age, he quickly rose through the ranks under the mentorship of his uncle, Shirkuh, a trusted general of the Zengid dynasty. Salah ad-Din's early career was marked by his service in Egypt, where he played a pivotal role in supporting the Fatimid Caliphate against internal and external threats.

Military Campaigns and Strategic Acumen

Salah ad-Din's military genius became evident through his numerous campaigns that expanded his influence across the Middle

East. One of his most notable early achievements was his participation in the campaigns against the Crusader states in the Levant. His ability to strategize and adapt to varying combat situations earned him a reputation as a formidable leader. Salah ad-Din's tactical innovations, such as his use of mobile cavalry units and siege warfare techniques, allowed him to secure significant victories against numerically superior foes.

Consolidation of Power in Egypt

In 1171, Salah ad-Din was appointed vizier of Egypt by the young Sultan al-Adid. Utilizing this position, he began consolidating power, effectively transforming Egypt into the center of his burgeoning empire. Salah ad-Din's governance in Egypt was marked by administrative reforms, economic stabilization, and the promotion of Sunni Islam, which helped unify the diverse populations under his rule. His ability to manage both the civilian and military aspects of his territories showcased his comprehensive leadership skills.

Unification of Muslim Territories

One of Salah ad-Din's most significant accomplishments was the unification of the Muslim territories in the face of the Crusader threat. By reconciling with rival factions and leveraging his diplomatic skills, he managed to bring together various leaders who were previously at odds. This unification was crucial in creating a cohesive front against the Crusaders, allowing Salah ad-Din to marshal resources effectively and coordinate large-scale military campaigns.

The Battle of Hattin and the Recapture of Jerusalem

The zenith of Salah ad-Din's military career came with the Battle of Hattin in 1187. Demonstrating strategic brilliance, he lured the Crusader forces into a vulnerable position near the Horns of Hattin, where his well-prepared army decimated the Crusaders, leading to the capture of key leaders and the subsequent fall of Jerusalem. This victory not only cemented his status as the preeminent Muslim leader of his time but also had profound implications for the balance of power in the region.

Rise to Prominence and Leadership Philosophy

Salah ad-Din's rise to prominence was not solely due to his military successes but also his leadership philosophy, which emphasized justice, compassion, and strategic wisdom. Unlike many of his contemporaries, he balanced martial prowess with ethical governance, earning him respect and loyalty from both his allies and adversaries. His ability to inspire and lead diverse groups towards a common goal was instrumental in his success and enduring legacy.

Impact on the Muslim World and Beyond

Salah ad-Din's leadership during the Crusades had a unifying effect on the Muslim world, fostering a sense of solidarity and purpose among disparate factions. His actions revitalized Islamic leadership and left an indelible mark on both Muslim and Christian narratives of the time. In the West, he was often portrayed as a noble and chivalrous adversary, a testament to his reputation for honor and integrity.

Conclusion of the Rise to Power

Salah ad-Din's rise from a provincial governor's son to the Sultan of Egypt and Syria exemplifies his exceptional leadership and strategic mind. His ability to navigate the complex political landscapes, unite diverse groups, and execute decisive military campaigns established him as a legendary figure in history. Understanding his ascent provides valuable insights into the principles of effective leadership, strategic planning, and ethical governance that are explored throughout *The Conqueror's Code*.

Key Themes to Highlight:

1. **Leadership from Humble Beginnings:** Emphasize how Salah ad-Din's early life and education laid the foundation for his later achievements.

2. **Strategic and Tactical Excellence:** Detail his military

campaigns, highlighting key battles and his ability to adapt strategies.

3. **Unification and Diplomacy:** Showcase his diplomatic efforts to unite the Muslim world against a common enemy.

4. **Ethical Leadership:** Illustrate how his commitment to justice and compassion set him apart from other military leaders.

5. **Legacy of Respect and Honor:** Discuss how his reputation for integrity and honor influenced both his contemporaries and future generations.

Potential Subsections:

- **Early Influences:** Explore the impact of his family background and early mentors on his development.

- **Key Military Campaigns:** Provide detailed accounts of significant battles and campaigns that propelled him to power.

- **Administrative Reforms in Egypt:** Examine his governance style and reforms that stabilized and strengthened his rule.

- **Diplomatic Strategies:** Analyze his methods for uniting rival factions and building alliances.

- **Cultural and Religious Impact:** Discuss his role in promoting Sunni Islam and his influence on the cultural landscape of his territories.

Historical Context:

To fully appreciate Salah ad-Din's rise, it's essential to understand the broader historical context of the 12th century Middle East, including the fragmentation of Muslim territories, the Crusader states' presence, and the political dynamics within the Islamic world. This background will provide readers with a comprehensive understanding of the challenges Salah ad-Din faced and how he overcame them.

His Enduring Influence

INFLUENCE IN THE ISLAMIC World

Salah ad-Din's legacy endures strongly within the Islamic world, where he is celebrated as a unifying leader, a model of justice, and an embodiment of chivalrous leadership. His efforts to defend Islamic lands during the Crusades and reclaim Jerusalem made him a symbol of resistance against foreign invasion and occupation. His name evokes deep respect across various Muslim cultures, as he is seen not only as a successful military leader but also as a pious ruler who upheld Islamic principles of justice, humility, and compassion.

- **The Unification of Muslim Lands**: Salah ad-Din's ability to unite the fractured Muslim world during a time of division is one of his most significant contributions. His efforts to reconcile different sects, ethnic groups, and rival dynasties inspired future leaders and scholars to pursue unity within the broader Muslim community, a goal that remains relevant in today's political landscape.

- **The Recapture of Jerusalem**: Salah ad-Din's recapture of Jerusalem in 1187 cemented his place in Islamic history as a liberator. For many Muslims, his victory is a powerful symbol of hope, resilience, and the triumph of faith. His respectful treatment of the city's Christian inhabitants after the conquest set an example of mercy in victory that resonated through generations.

- **A Model for Ethical Leadership**: Salah ad-Din's rule is often highlighted as a golden standard of Islamic governance. He balanced military strength with a deep commitment to justice, earning him a revered status in

Islamic history. His actions reflect the Quranic values of fairness and compassion, making him a figure whom both scholars and everyday Muslims look up to when discussing Islamic rulership and leadership.

Influence in the Western World

Remarkably, Salah ad-Din's reputation also extended beyond the Muslim world, earning him the admiration of his Christian foes, particularly in Europe. In Western medieval literature and history, Salah ad-Din became a symbol of chivalry and nobility, qualities often attributed to idealized knights. Despite the intense conflict between the Christian and Muslim worlds during the Crusades, Salah ad-Din's conduct inspired respect, admiration, and even admiration from his enemies.

- **Chivalric Respect**: During the Third Crusade, despite being adversaries, both Salah ad-Din and King Richard the Lionheart developed mutual respect for each other. Western chronicles from the time speak of Salah ad-Din's generosity in offering medical aid to Richard when he fell ill during the campaign, highlighting the chivalrous values that defined Salah ad-Din's leadership. This act of generosity, along with his mercy toward Christians after retaking Jerusalem, helped craft an image of him as a noble warrior in European literature.

- **A Figure in European Literature**: Salah ad-Din's legend grew not only in historical records but also in medieval European literature. He became a model of the idealized "Saracen" leader, embodying wisdom, magnanimity, and military prowess. His portrayal in works such as Dante Alighieri's *The Divine Comedy* placed him among the "virtuous pagans" in Limbo, alongside great figures from history and philosophy, a testament to his enduring impact on the Western imagination.

- **Salah ad-Din as a Model of Tolerance**: In the centuries following his death, Salah ad-Din's legacy in the West evolved into one of tolerance and cross-cultural respect. His mercy toward Christians and Jews after the conquest of Jerusalem contrasted sharply with the violent actions of many Crusader leaders, marking him as a figure of ethical governance and religious tolerance. Today, he is often referenced in the West as a historical model for peaceful coexistence and mutual respect between different cultures and religions.

Relevance of His Leadership Today

Salah ad-Din's principles of leadership, particularly his focus on justice, compassion, and unity, remain highly relevant in modern times. In an era marked by political division, social upheaval, and conflict, the example he set offers timeless lessons for leaders and individuals alike. His ability to balance strength with mercy, to act with strategic patience, and to inspire unity in the face of division can serve as a blueprint for effective leadership in various contexts, from governance to business and personal development.

- **The Power of Ethical Leadership**: Salah ad-Din's reign exemplifies how ethical leadership can create lasting respect and legitimacy. Modern leaders, whether in politics, business, or community organizations, can look to his example of leading with integrity, compassion, and justice. His legacy demonstrates that success can be achieved not only through power but also through moral authority.

- **Unity in Diversity**: In a time of fragmented political landscapes and societal divisions, Salah ad-Din's ability to unite different factions for a common cause provides valuable lessons in coalition-building and conflict resolution. His methods of bringing rival groups together while respecting their differences remain applicable to leaders facing diverse constituencies today.

- **Compassion in Victory**: In today's competitive world, where victory often leads to the marginalization or exploitation of the defeated, Salah ad-Din's example of showing mercy even in conquest serves as a reminder that true strength lies in compassion. His actions demonstrate that leaders who act with humility and kindness leave a more enduring and respected legacy.

- **Balancing Faith and Leadership**: Salah ad-Din's ability to integrate his personal faith into his leadership without alienating those of other beliefs offers a model for modern leaders navigating multicultural environments. His respect for religious diversity while remaining firm in his own convictions is a key takeaway for those leading in a globalized world.

Salah ad-Din's Global Legacy

Salah ad-Din's influence extends far beyond his time and region. His legacy is not confined to the history books but continues to inspire leaders, scholars, and individuals seeking a model of ethical and effective leadership. He is celebrated not just for his victories on the battlefield, but for the way he wielded power with restraint, wisdom, and compassion. As a global symbol of honorable leadership, his legacy transcends the divisions of his time and speaks to the universal values of justice, unity, and respect for humanity.

- **Influence on Modern Leadership Studies**: Salah ad-Din's life and leadership have been studied in military academies and leadership programs around the world. His ability to blend tactical acumen with emotional intelligence and ethical governance serves as a case study in how to lead effectively while remaining true to one's values.

- **Symbol of Interfaith Dialogue**: In contemporary times, Salah ad-Din is often invoked as a historical figure who exemplified respect for religious differences. His legacy is referenced in efforts to promote interfaith dialogue and cooperation, particularly between the Muslim and Christian worlds.

Conclusion of His Enduring Influence

Salah ad-Din's legacy endures because he embodied the qualities of a true leader—justice, compassion, strength, and wisdom. His ability to inspire both his followers and his adversaries speaks to the universal appeal of his leadership style. Today, as the world grapples with new challenges, the lessons from Salah ad-Din's life offer valuable insights into how we can lead with integrity, unify divided groups, and wield power with mercy and wisdom. His life's work continues to resonate not only in the Islamic world but across cultures and time, making him a timeless figure of leadership for all generations.

Purpose of the Book

THE PRIMARY AIM OF *The Conqueror's Code: Salah ad-Din's Principles for Life and Leadership* is to distill the timeless lessons from Salah ad-Din's life and leadership into practical strategies that readers can apply in their own lives. His principles—rooted in justice, compassion, strategic wisdom, and ethical governance—are as relevant today as they were during his time. Whether the reader is a leader in the business world, a community organizer, or simply someone seeking personal growth, the insights gained from Salah ad-Din's example can serve as a powerful guide for facing modern challenges.

Applying Salah ad-Din's Leadership Principles in Modern Life

Salah ad-Din's leadership style was defined by his ability to inspire loyalty, unify divided groups, and lead with both strength and compassion. In today's world, where individuals and leaders often face similar challenges of division, competition, and ethical dilemmas, his approach offers valuable lessons that transcend time and culture.

- **Strategic Leadership in a Complex World**: Salah ad-Din mastered the art of balancing long-term goals with short-term actions. His ability to maintain focus on his broader mission—reclaiming Jerusalem—while managing daily political, military, and administrative tasks is a model for strategic leadership. In modern settings, whether in business or governance, leaders face similar complexity. Salah ad-Din's method of prioritizing goals, staying patient, and executing decisive actions when the time is right offers a timeless lesson for navigating today's dynamic environments.

- **Leading with Compassion and Strength**: One of Salah ad-Din's defining characteristics was his ability to lead with a blend of compassion and strength. In today's competitive world, many leaders struggle to balance toughness with empathy. This book seeks to explore how Salah ad-Din's merciful approach, even toward his adversaries, can be applied by modern leaders to build stronger, more resilient teams. Readers will learn how compassion is not a sign of weakness, but a powerful tool for fostering loyalty and respect.

Personal Growth Through Salah ad-Din's Code

Salah ad-Din's personal traits of humility, self-discipline, and perseverance serve as a blueprint for individuals striving to grow in their personal lives. His rise to power was not marked by ruthless ambition but by his dedication to service, faith, and justice. This book will guide readers in applying these principles to their personal journeys, helping them to face challenges with resilience and integrity.

- **Patience and Perseverance in Adversity**: Salah ad-Din's strategic patience, especially in the long lead-up to the recapture of Jerusalem, teaches the importance of perseverance when faced with obstacles. In a fast-paced world that often emphasizes quick wins, his example reminds us that true success requires patience and endurance. This principle can be applied to personal goals, relationships, or any area of life where setbacks are common.

- **Living with Integrity**: Salah ad-Din's commitment to justice and his refusal to betray his values, even in the face of immense pressure, provides a powerful model for how individuals can live with integrity in today's world. Whether in professional settings or personal relationships, readers will learn the importance of standing firm in their principles, even when it's difficult.

Practical Applications for Modern Leaders and Individuals

The book will also offer concrete strategies for how to implement Salah ad-Din's principles in everyday life. Each chapter will present actionable steps that readers can take to become better leaders, improve their decision-making, and cultivate personal growth.

- **Building Trust and Loyalty**: Salah ad-Din was renowned for the loyalty he inspired among his soldiers and allies. By exploring his methods of earning trust through transparency, fairness, and leading by example, the book will show how readers can foster loyalty in their own teams, organizations, or relationships.

- **Navigating Conflict with Honor**: Salah ad-Din's conduct in warfare, particularly his respect for his enemies, offers modern readers a guide to handling conflict with honor and integrity. This principle can be applied to professional disputes, competitive business environments, or even personal conflicts, where the goal is not just to win but to do so with dignity.

Life Challenges: Facing Modern Struggles with Salah ad-Din's Wisdom

The wisdom drawn from Salah ad-Din's life extends beyond leadership and personal development. The challenges he faced—ranging from political betrayal to military setbacks—mirror the kinds of struggles people face today, whether in their careers or personal lives. This book will offer insights into how his responses to adversity can guide readers in overcoming their own challenges.

- **Handling Failure with Grace**: Salah ad-Din's career was not without setbacks, but his ability to rebound from defeats and learn from his mistakes was key to his eventual success.

The book will discuss how readers can adopt a similar mindset, treating failures as opportunities for growth rather than reasons for despair.

● **Balancing Ambition with Ethical Boundaries**: While Salah ad-Din was undoubtedly ambitious, he consistently acted within the boundaries of his ethical and moral convictions. In a world where ambition can sometimes lead to compromising one's values, his example offers a roadmap for achieving success without sacrificing integrity.

Conclusion of Purpose

Ultimately, *The Conqueror's Code* aims to show readers that Salah ad-Din's principles are not relics of the past, but practical tools for navigating the complexities of modern life. Whether you are leading a team, managing a business, or striving for personal growth, this book will help you apply the wisdom of one of history's greatest leaders to your own challenges. By embracing Salah ad-Din's code of leadership, justice, and compassion, readers will be better equipped to lead with honor, face adversity with resilience, and build a lasting legacy of their own.

Part I: The Pillars of Leadership

Chapter 1: Unity of Purpose

Historical Insight: How Salah ad-Din United a Fractured Muslim World to Repel the Crusaders

The Fractured State of the Muslim World

In the mid-12th century, when Salah ad-Din rose to power, the Muslim world was deeply divided. The Abbasid Caliphate, once the unifying force of Islam, had lost much of its influence and authority. Political fragmentation, dynastic rivalries, and religious sectarianism had created internal divisions across the Muslim lands. The Fatimid Caliphate in Egypt, the Seljuks in Anatolia and Persia, the Zengid rulers in Syria, and various other local powers operated as independent states or mini-kingdoms, often at odds with each other. This lack of unity made the Muslim world vulnerable to external threats, particularly from the Crusaders, who had established a foothold in the Levant with the Kingdom of Jerusalem and other Crusader states.

Salah ad-Din's Diplomatic Skill: The Key to Unification

Salah ad-Din recognized that to effectively repel the Crusaders and secure the long-term defense of Islamic territories, the Muslim world needed unity. Rather than relying solely on military conquest to bring rival factions together, Salah ad-Din used his diplomatic acumen to forge alliances and cultivate loyalty across a fractured political landscape.

- **Marriage Alliances and Political Ties**: Salah ad-Din strategically used marriage alliances to strengthen ties with powerful Muslim families and tribes. For example, he married the niece of Nur ad-Din, his former master and the ruler of Syria, which cemented his claim to leadership in Syria after Nur ad-Din's death. This approach of building familial ties helped Salah ad-Din secure the loyalty of key allies who might otherwise have challenged his authority.

- **Negotiation and Reconciliation**: Salah ad-Din was adept at negotiating peace and reconciliation between rival Muslim factions. He avoided unnecessary conflicts with other Muslim leaders whenever possible, preferring diplomacy to force. His ability to resolve disputes and offer favorable terms to rivals helped him integrate these factions into his broader coalition without alienating them. For instance, when he took over Egypt, he did so with minimal bloodshed and worked to peacefully dissolve the Fatimid Caliphate, bringing Egypt firmly under his control without inciting a rebellion.

Uniting Sunni and Shia Factions

One of Salah ad-Din's most significant accomplishments was his ability to bridge the divide between Sunni and Shia Muslims. Egypt, under Fatimid rule, had been the seat of Shia power, while Salah ad-Din and his supporters were staunch Sunnis. Rather than ruthlessly suppressing the Shia population, he gradually transitioned Egypt back into the Sunni fold through a combination of administrative reforms and religious policies. He replaced Shia officials with Sunni administrators and scholars but did so gradually and peacefully, avoiding outright persecution of the Shia population.

This careful approach helped Salah ad-Din avoid alienating a large segment of the Muslim population and ensured that Egypt remained stable under his rule. By focusing on shared goals—defending Muslim lands from the Crusaders—rather than exacerbating sectarian divides, he fostered a sense of unity that transcended religious differences.

Cultivating Loyalty Across Ethnic and Political Divides

Salah ad-Din's ability to inspire loyalty across different ethnic groups and political factions was another critical factor in his success. His army was a multi-ethnic force, composed of Kurds (like himself), Turks, Arabs, and other ethnic groups. Rather than playing one group against another, as many leaders of the time did, Salah ad-Din treated his soldiers and commanders with respect, regardless of their background. He ensured that loyalty to him was based on merit and shared purpose rather than ethnic or tribal identity.

- **Fairness and Justice**: One of the reasons Salah ad-Din was able to command such loyalty was his reputation for fairness and justice. He distributed spoils of war equitably among his soldiers and rewarded merit rather than favoritism. His sense of justice made him a respected leader, and many of his rivals eventually aligned with him because they trusted his leadership.

- **Inclusion and Empowerment of Local Leaders**: Salah ad-Din often worked with local leaders rather than imposing direct rule over them. He allowed many of his allies to retain control over their regions as long as they pledged loyalty to him and contributed to the larger goal of defending against the Crusaders. This decentralized approach enabled him to build a coalition of semi-autonomous rulers who remained loyal because they benefited from his leadership.

Military Campaigns: A Unifying Cause

The Crusades provided a common enemy that Salah ad-Din could use to unite the Muslim world. He framed his campaigns not just as territorial conquests but as a religious duty—a jihad to protect Islamic lands and reclaim Jerusalem from Christian control. By positioning himself as the defender of Islam and the liberator of Jerusalem, Salah ad-Din rallied Muslim leaders and soldiers around a unifying cause that transcended their individual rivalries.

- **Symbolism of Jerusalem**: The recapture of Jerusalem became the central goal of Salah ad-Din's campaigns. The city's religious significance to Muslims made it a rallying point that could inspire even his most reluctant allies to join his cause. Jerusalem was not just a strategic objective but a symbol of Islamic unity and resistance against foreign invaders.

The Battle of Hattin: The Culmination of Unity

The Battle of Hattin in 1187 was the crowning achievement of Salah ad-Din's efforts to unite the Muslim world. By this time, he had successfully brought together a vast coalition of Muslim forces from Egypt, Syria, and other regions. The battle itself was a masterpiece of strategic coordination and cooperation among these diverse forces. Salah ad-Din's army decisively defeated the Crusader forces, capturing key leaders and paving the way for the recapture of Jerusalem.

The victory at Hattin was the result of years of patient diplomacy, alliance-building, and military preparation. It demonstrated how unity of purpose could overcome even the most powerful enemies. The battle also solidified Salah ad-Din's reputation as the preeminent leader of the Muslim world, further consolidating his power and influence.

Legacy of Unity and Leadership

Salah ad-Din's ability to unite the Muslim world had lasting effects. After his death, the Muslim territories he unified remained relatively stable for several decades, and his example of leadership became a model for future Muslim rulers. His focus on unity, diplomacy, and justice left an enduring legacy that resonates in the Islamic world to this day.

Lessons for Modern Leaders

For modern leaders, Salah ad-Din's unification of the Muslim world offers valuable lessons in diplomacy, coalition-building, and the importance of a unifying cause. His ability to navigate complex political landscapes, reconcile opposing factions, and inspire loyalty across ethnic and religious divides demonstrates the power of leadership that is rooted in justice, respect, and shared purpose. In today's world, where divisions and conflicts often arise within organizations, communities, or nations, Salah ad-Din's approach provides a timeless blueprint for achieving unity and overcoming fragmentation.

Lesson for Today: Unifying Teams with a Common Goal

SALAH AD-DIN'S ABILITY to unify the Muslim world against the Crusaders offers powerful lessons for modern leaders who are tasked with bringing together diverse teams, navigating internal divisions, and fostering collaboration toward a shared objective. Whether leading in the corporate world, managing a nonprofit, or guiding a community group, leaders today face the same challenge that Salah ad-Din did—creating unity in the face of competing interests, cultures, and perspectives. Here are key lessons that can be applied in today's leadership contexts:

1. Define and Focus on a Unifying Goal

HISTORICAL LESSON: Salah ad-Din's unification efforts succeeded because he provided a clear, unifying goal that transcended individual and factional interests—the recapture of Jerusalem and the defense of Islamic lands. By emphasizing a higher purpose, he was able to rally diverse groups that might otherwise have been in conflict with each other.

Modern Application: Leaders today must articulate a common, overarching goal that unites their teams or organizations. This goal should be clear, inspiring, and significant enough to motivate individuals to set aside personal differences or competing agendas. In business, this could be a vision for the future of the company or a transformative project that everyone can contribute to. In a nonprofit or community organization, it might be a social cause that resonates with all members. The key is to focus everyone's attention on a shared purpose that creates a sense of belonging and collective effort.

- **Example**: In a company undergoing restructuring, the CEO might emphasize the goal of becoming the industry leader in innovation, inspiring teams to collaborate across departments to achieve this vision. By uniting everyone around a common purpose, individual concerns about restructuring can be alleviated by a sense of working toward something greater.

---

2. Build Trust and Loyalty Through Fairness and Respect

HISTORICAL LESSON: Salah ad-Din cultivated loyalty among diverse groups by treating people fairly, rewarding merit, and showing respect for different cultures, ethnicities, and religious beliefs. He demonstrated that loyalty is earned, not demanded, and that trust is built over time through just and respectful leadership.

Modern Application: In today's organizations, leaders must earn the loyalty of their teams by creating an environment of fairness and respect. This means acknowledging and valuing the contributions of all team members, regardless of their background or position. Leaders should also ensure that rewards, promotions, and recognition are based on merit rather than favoritism or bias.

- **Example**: A manager overseeing a team of employees from diverse cultural backgrounds might take the time to understand each person's unique strengths and challenges. By listening to their concerns, offering equal opportunities for growth, and celebrating their successes, the manager builds a foundation of trust and loyalty within the team.

3. Use Diplomacy to Navigate Differences

HISTORICAL LESSON: Salah ad-Din was a master of diplomacy, often choosing negotiation over confrontation when dealing with rival Muslim factions. He understood that unity could not be achieved through force alone and that reconciliation and compromise were often more effective in maintaining long-term stability.

Modern Application: In today's organizations, leaders must use diplomacy to navigate conflicts and differences within their teams. Rather than imposing top-down decisions, they should encourage open dialogue, seek input from all stakeholders, and work toward solutions that satisfy everyone's interests. Compromise and negotiation are essential tools in unifying a team and maintaining harmony.

- **Example**: In a company experiencing tension between two departments due to differing priorities, a leader might bring both teams together to openly discuss their challenges and find a compromise. By facilitating collaboration and ensuring that each side's concerns are addressed, the leader fosters a more cooperative environment and reduces internal friction.

4. Foster Inclusivity and Collaboration Across Divides

HISTORICAL LESSON: Salah ad-Din's army was composed of soldiers and commanders from various ethnic and religious backgrounds, yet he fostered unity by creating a sense of shared identity and purpose. He encouraged collaboration and inclusivity, ensuring that all voices were heard and that the strengths of different groups were leveraged.

Modern Application: Leaders today must create an inclusive environment where team members from diverse backgrounds feel valued and empowered to contribute. This requires fostering a culture of collaboration, where individuals with different perspectives work together toward common goals. Leaders should actively encourage cross-functional teamwork and diversity of thought, as this can lead to more innovative and effective solutions.

- **Example**: A company focused on developing a new product might create cross-departmental teams that bring together engineers, designers, marketers, and customer support representatives. By encouraging collaboration between departments that typically work in silos, the company can create a product that benefits from a range of expertise and perspectives, leading to better results.

---

5. Demonstrate Compassion and Empathy

HISTORICAL LESSON: Salah ad-Din was known not only for his military prowess but also for his compassion and empathy, even toward his enemies. His ability to show mercy, despite being a formidable leader, earned him respect from both allies and adversaries. This compassion helped him foster unity by demonstrating that leadership is not just about power but also about understanding and care for others.

Modern Application: In today's world, leaders who show empathy toward their team members are more likely to create a loyal and motivated workforce. Understanding the personal challenges and needs of individuals, and responding with kindness and flexibility, can strengthen relationships and build a sense of unity. Compassionate leadership also involves supporting team members through difficult times and showing a genuine interest in their well-being.

- **Example**: A leader who notices that an employee is struggling with a heavy workload might offer additional resources or extend deadlines to ease the pressure. By showing empathy and addressing the employee's challenges, the leader not only helps the individual but also strengthens team morale, as others see that their leader genuinely cares about their well-being.

6. Be Patient and Strategic in Pursuing Long-Term Goals

HISTORICAL LESSON: Salah ad-Din was known for his patience and long-term strategic planning. He didn't rush into battles or make impulsive decisions; instead, he carefully considered the broader picture and waited for the right moment to act. This patience allowed him to avoid unnecessary conflicts and maximize his chances of success in uniting the Muslim world.

Modern Application: Leaders today must recognize that unifying a team or achieving a major goal takes time. Impulsive decisions or short-term thinking can undermine long-term success. Instead, leaders should adopt a patient, strategic approach, focusing on incremental progress and carefully timed actions. This also means being patient with team members as they grow and develop, allowing them to contribute meaningfully over time.

- **Example**: A CEO leading a company through a major transformation might avoid making drastic changes all at once, instead implementing a phased approach. By focusing on smaller, achievable milestones, the CEO allows the organization to adapt at a sustainable pace, building unity and buy-in from employees over time.

Conclusion: Embracing Unity in Leadership Today

MODERN LEADERS CAN learn a great deal from Salah ad-Din's approach to unifying a divided world. By defining a clear and inspiring goal, building trust through fairness and respect, using diplomacy to navigate differences, fostering inclusivity and collaboration, demonstrating compassion, and exercising patience in pursuit of long-term success, leaders can cultivate a strong sense of unity within their teams and organizations.

The lessons from Salah ad-Din's life are not limited to the battlefield or political leadership; they are equally relevant in today's workplaces, communities, and personal relationships. By applying these principles, modern leaders can inspire loyalty, resolve conflicts, and guide their teams toward a common purpose, just as Salah ad-Din united the Muslim world to achieve great victories against formidable odds.

Chapter 2: Leading by Example

Historical Insight: Salah ad-Din's Leadership from the Front

Salah ad-Din's rise to legendary status was not solely due to his strategic brilliance or military prowess. His real strength lay in his ability to lead from the front, both on the battlefield and in daily life. By sharing the hardships and rewards of his soldiers and subjects, he earned their unwavering loyalty and respect. This leadership style, grounded in humility and personal sacrifice, was critical in shaping Salah ad-Din's reputation as one of history's most admired leaders.

Leadership on the Battlefield

Salah ad-Din's reputation as a military commander was solidified through his presence on the front lines during critical battles. Unlike many rulers of his time, who directed operations from the rear or in the safety of distant fortresses, Salah ad-Din was often seen fighting shoulder to shoulder with his troops. His personal bravery and active participation in the heat of battle inspired his men to fight with greater courage, knowing their leader was facing the same dangers.

- **At the Battle of Hattin (1187)**: This decisive victory over the Crusaders is one of the most vivid examples of Salah ad-Din leading from the front. He did not merely command his forces; he was physically present, directing the assault, and rallying his men with personal leadership. His ability to remain composed and strategically decisive during this critical moment was a key factor in the crushing defeat of the Crusader forces, leading to the eventual recapture of Jerusalem.

- **Inspiring His Troops**: Salah ad-Din's active involvement on the battlefield served to motivate his soldiers, who admired his courage and willingness to share in their risks. His soldiers did not fight for a distant ruler; they fought for a leader who stood beside them in the face of danger. This personal connection to his men fostered deep loyalty and commitment, as they knew their leader was as invested in their survival and success as they were.

Humility and Shared Hardships

Salah ad-Din's leadership extended beyond battle tactics; he embodied humility in his everyday life. Despite his immense power as the ruler of Egypt and Syria, he lived modestly and shared the same conditions as his soldiers, especially during campaigns. He ate the same food, slept in the same conditions, and refrained from the luxury that was typical for a man of his stature.

- **Living as One of His Soldiers**: During military campaigns, Salah ad-Din made it a point to share in the same hardships as his troops. He rejected the comforts that could have easily been provided to him and chose instead to sleep in tents, eat simple meals, and endure the fatigue of long marches. This deepened the bond between him and his soldiers, who saw him as not just a ruler, but a comrade who was willing to endure the same struggles for the greater cause.

- **Rewarding Loyalty Fairly**: Salah ad-Din also ensured that the rewards of victory were shared equally among his men. After major victories, such as the capture of Jerusalem, he distributed the spoils of war in a manner that reflected fairness and justice. His soldiers and commanders were generously compensated for their efforts, further solidifying their loyalty and respect for him. This practice contrasted with many contemporary rulers, who often kept the lion's share of the spoils for themselves.

Gaining Respect Through Personal Sacrifice

Salah ad-Din's humility extended to his personal possessions and lifestyle. While he had access to vast wealth and could have lived in luxury, he chose a simple life. This humility set him apart from many rulers of the time and contributed to his reputation for justice and fairness. His personal sacrifices were a testament to his belief in leadership as service, a principle that resonated with both his subjects and his enemies.

- **A Humble Ruler**: Despite ruling a vast empire, Salah ad-Din was known for his lack of personal wealth at the time of his death. He had given much of his wealth away to support his troops, build infrastructure, and assist the poor. This selflessness earned him admiration not only from his followers but also from those who opposed him. Even Richard the Lionheart, his great adversary during the Crusades, spoke of him with respect.

- **Mercy Toward Enemies**: Salah ad-Din's humility and sense of justice extended to his treatment of enemies. After the recapture of Jerusalem, he allowed Christian civilians to leave the city unharmed, contrasting sharply with the brutal massacres that had occurred when the Crusaders initially took the city in 1099. His decision to show mercy was not only an act of compassion but a demonstration of his belief in leading through justice and moral authority.

Everyday Conduct and Governance

Salah ad-Din's leadership by example wasn't confined to the battlefield; it was reflected in his governance as well. He approached rulership with the same humility, justice, and compassion that he exhibited in war. His fairness in administering justice and his dedication to the well-being of his subjects earned him respect not just as a military leader, but as a ruler who genuinely cared for his people.

- **Justice for All**: Salah ad-Din was committed to upholding justice in all aspects of his rule. His legal reforms, which sought to ensure fairness and equity in the treatment of his subjects, earned him a reputation as a just ruler. He did not differentiate between his people based on their ethnicity, religion, or social status, and he was known to intervene personally in cases where he believed injustice was being done.

- **Serving the People**: Salah ad-Din's leadership philosophy centered around the idea that rulers were meant to serve the people, not dominate them. This approach was reflected in his efforts to improve infrastructure, build schools, and ensure the prosperity of his lands. His actions inspired a sense of trust and loyalty among his subjects, who saw him as a ruler who genuinely cared for their well-being.

Impact of Leadership by Example

Salah ad-Din's leadership style—leading from the front, sharing in hardships, and embodying humility—had a profound and lasting impact. His ability to command both respect and loyalty from his soldiers and subjects alike was rooted in the fact that he did not see himself as above them, but as one of them. His actions spoke louder than words, and it was through these actions that he built an unshakable bond with those he led.

Chapter 2: Leading by Example

Lesson for Today: Leadership through Integrity, Accountability, and Sacrifice

IN TODAY'S FAST-PACED world, where trust in leadership is often fragile, the principles that Salah ad-Din embodied—integrity, accountability, and personal sacrifice—remain essential for cultivating respect and loyalty. Modern leaders, whether in business, politics, or personal endeavors, can learn from his example that the most effective way to lead is by living the values they wish to instill in others. Leadership today is not about giving commands from a distance, but about demonstrating integrity through personal action and earning respect by walking the same path as those you lead.

1. Setting a Personal Example with Integrity

HISTORICAL INSIGHT: Salah ad-Din's integrity was a cornerstone of his leadership. He lived simply, treated people fairly, and avoided the luxury and greed that often corrupted other leaders of his time. His troops and subjects admired him not just for his military skill but for his honesty and adherence to principles of justice.

Modern Application: Integrity remains the foundation of effective leadership. Leaders today must demonstrate a commitment to ethical behavior, fairness, and transparency in all their actions. Integrity is not just about avoiding unethical conduct but about consistently making decisions that align with one's values, even when it is difficult. Modern leaders should act with honesty in both success and failure, earning the trust of those they lead by staying true to their principles.

- **Example**: A CEO who takes responsibility for a failed project instead of blaming the team demonstrates integrity and accountability. This not only builds trust but also encourages a culture of openness, where employees feel safe to take risks and learn from mistakes.

2. Practicing Accountability in Leadership

HISTORICAL INSIGHT: Salah ad-Din held himself accountable to his troops and his people. He did not separate himself from the consequences of his decisions, whether they led to success or failure. By sharing in both the hardships and the rewards, he made it clear that he was as responsible as anyone for the outcomes of his actions.

Modern Application: Accountability is crucial in modern leadership. Leaders must be willing to accept responsibility for their actions and decisions, especially when things go wrong. This means owning mistakes, learning from them, and showing others that you are committed to continuous improvement. Leaders who demonstrate accountability foster a culture of responsibility within their teams, where everyone feels empowered to take ownership of their roles.

- **Example**: A manager who publicly acknowledges a misstep and outlines steps to improve not only models accountability but also encourages team members to take responsibility for their work without fear of undue blame.

3. Leading through Personal Sacrifice

HISTORICAL INSIGHT: Salah ad-Din's leadership was defined by personal sacrifice. He lived and fought alongside his soldiers, enduring the same hardships and dangers. His willingness to sacrifice comfort, safety, and personal gain for the greater good earned him the respect and loyalty of those he led. He led by action, not just by words, which made his leadership genuine and impactful.

Modern Application: In today's world, leaders must show a willingness to sacrifice for the well-being of their teams, organizations, or communities. This might mean putting in extra effort during challenging times, giving up personal benefits to ensure the success of the group, or stepping back to allow others to shine. Leadership requires service, and those who are willing to make personal sacrifices for the greater good build lasting respect and loyalty.

- **Example**: During economic downturns, a leader who voluntarily takes a pay cut to avoid laying off employees demonstrates personal sacrifice and shows the team that their well-being is a top priority.

---

4. Cultivating Respect through Personal Action

HISTORICAL INSIGHT: Salah ad-Din didn't just give orders; he led by example. Whether on the battlefield or in daily governance, he demonstrated the qualities he expected from his followers. His soldiers respected him because they saw him enduring the same struggles, and his subjects admired him because he treated them with fairness and humility.

Modern Application: Leaders today must realize that respect is not demanded but earned through consistent personal action. Words alone are not enough to inspire loyalty—actions speak louder. Leaders who demonstrate the values they want to see in their teams, such as hard work, empathy, and resilience, set the standard for others to follow. By leading through personal example, leaders build credibility and trust.

- **Example**: A team leader who stays late to help finish a project or steps in to support an overworked colleague shows that they are willing to share the burden. This action not only fosters respect but also motivates others to follow suit and work collaboratively.

---

5. Building a Culture of Trust through Authentic Leadership

HISTORICAL INSIGHT: Salah ad-Din's authenticity as a leader, grounded in his humility and honesty, was key to building trust with his troops and subjects. His leadership was genuine, and people followed him not out of fear or obligation, but out of loyalty and admiration for his character.

Modern Application: Trust is the cornerstone of modern leadership. Authentic leaders who are open about their values, transparent in their decision-making, and willing to admit vulnerabilities are more likely to gain the trust of their teams. By showing up as their true selves and aligning their actions with their words, modern leaders can cultivate deep trust and loyalty.

- **Example**: A leader who is open about the challenges the organization is facing, while also providing a clear plan and rallying the team around a shared goal, creates an environment of trust. Employees are more likely to follow someone who is genuine and transparent, even in difficult times.

---

6. Inspiring Others to Emulate Leadership Values

HISTORICAL INSIGHT: Salah ad-Din inspired those around him to embody the values he lived by—justice, compassion, and courage.

His leadership style created a ripple effect, as his commanders, soldiers, and subjects sought to mirror his actions in their own lives.

Modern Application: A key role of modern leaders is to inspire others to adopt the values they promote. By consistently modeling the behavior they expect, leaders can influence the culture of their organizations. When leaders demonstrate empathy, perseverance, and integrity, they set the tone for the entire team to follow, fostering a positive and productive environment.

- **Example**: A leader who consistently acts with integrity, even when faced with difficult choices, inspires team members to do the same in their work and interactions. Over time, this builds a culture where honesty and ethical behavior are the norm.

Conclusion: Leadership as a Reflection of Personal Values

IN TODAY'S WORLD, WHERE leadership is often measured by results and authority, Salah ad-Din's example serves as a powerful reminder that true leadership comes from within. Leaders who embody integrity, accountability, and personal sacrifice not only achieve success but also earn the lasting respect and loyalty of those they lead. By living the values they wish to instill in others, modern leaders can create environments of trust, collaboration, and mutual respect, much like Salah ad-Din did centuries ago.

Leadership by example isn't about grand gestures or authoritative commands—it's about the everyday actions that reflect a leader's commitment to their people and their principles. Whether in business, community leadership, or personal life, the lessons from Salah ad-Din's life remain timeless: lead with humility, act with integrity, and always be willing to make personal sacrifices for the greater good.

Chapter 3: The Power of Compassion

Historical Insight: Salah ad-Din's Compassion and Mercy Toward His Adversaries

Salah ad-Din, known for his fierce military leadership and strategic brilliance, was equally renowned for his compassion and mercy, even toward his adversaries. His ability to balance strength in warfare with humanity in victory set him apart from many leaders of his time. While he was a formidable warrior, his acts of mercy, particularly toward prisoners and defeated foes, demonstrated a deep commitment to justice and ethical leadership. One of the most remarkable examples of this was his treatment of the Christian inhabitants of Jerusalem after its recapture in 1187, a moment that highlighted his sense of moral responsibility and fairness.

The Fall of Jerusalem and the Treatment of Christians

THE SIEGE AND SURRENDER of Jerusalem (1187): After the decisive Muslim victory at the Battle of Hattin, Salah ad-Din's forces moved to retake Jerusalem from the Crusaders. The siege lasted for several days, and with the city surrounded and its defenders unable to mount a sustained resistance, it became clear that Jerusalem would fall. Given the bloody history of Jerusalem's conquests, particularly the massacre of Muslims and Jews by Crusaders during their capture of the city in 1099, many feared that Salah ad-Din would seek revenge in the same manner.

However, Salah ad-Din took a different approach. Instead of exacting brutal retribution, he showed remarkable clemency toward the city's Christian population, offering them safe passage and fair terms for their surrender. This act of mercy, especially given the historical context, cemented his reputation as a just and compassionate leader.

- **The Terms of Surrender**: Rather than slaughtering or enslaving the Christian population, Salah ad-Din allowed the inhabitants of Jerusalem to leave the city peacefully in exchange for a modest ransom. Those who could not pay were not abandoned—Salah ad-Din's own brother, Al-Adil, requested that several thousand poor Christians be allowed to leave without ransom, a request Salah ad-Din granted. This act of compassion provided safety for people who otherwise would have faced a grim fate.

- **Preserving Holy Sites**: Salah ad-Din's respect extended to religious sites as well. He ensured that Christian holy sites, including the Church of the Holy Sepulchre, were protected and that Christians would retain access to them for pilgrimage. This level of tolerance, especially during a period of religious warfare, demonstrated his commitment to coexistence and respect for other faiths.

Contrast with the Crusader Massacres: Salah ad-Din's mercy was in stark contrast to the actions of the Crusaders when they first took Jerusalem in 1099. During that conquest, Christian forces massacred thousands of Muslims and Jews, sparing neither women nor children. Salah ad-Din's restraint and compassion, therefore, were not simply military decisions but reflected his character and belief in the principles of justice and mercy. His actions earned him the respect of not only Muslims but also many Christians who recognized his fairness.

Mercy Toward Prisoners of War

SALAH AD-DIN'S COMPASSION extended beyond the fall of Jerusalem. Throughout his campaigns, he showed mercy toward prisoners of war, including prominent Crusader leaders. His treatment of captured knights and nobles, many of whom would have been executed by other leaders, was marked by honor and respect.

- **Ransom Instead of Execution**: Instead of killing prisoners, Salah ad-Din often ransomed them back to their own people, allowing them to return home. This practice was common in medieval warfare, but Salah ad-Din was particularly known for ensuring that prisoners were treated humanely, regardless of their rank or role in the conflict. His decision to spare the lives of many Crusader knights after the Battle of Hattin, for example, demonstrated his commitment to mercy even in victory.

- **The Case of King Guy of Lusignan**: After the Battle of Hattin, Salah ad-Din captured King Guy of Lusignan, the king of Jerusalem, along with several other high-ranking Crusader leaders. Rather than executing them, which would have been a significant blow to the Crusader cause, Salah ad-Din treated them with dignity and eventually released them. His decision to spare King Guy's life, despite the king's role in provoking the conflict, showcased Salah ad-Din's ability to balance justice with mercy.

Compassion Toward Civilians

SALAH AD-DIN'S COMPASSION was not limited to his treatment of military prisoners and leaders; he also demonstrated great care for civilians, even those who were not his subjects. Throughout his campaigns, he sought to minimize harm to non-combatants and to ensure that civilians, regardless of their religious or ethnic background, were treated with fairness and respect.

- **Protecting Civilians During Sieges**: During many of Salah ad-Din's sieges and military campaigns, he issued orders to spare civilians wherever possible. Unlike many military leaders of his time, who often saw the destruction of civilian populations as a necessary part of warfare, Salah ad-Din made efforts to protect non-combatants, especially women, children, and the elderly. His treatment of the civilian population during the recapture of Jerusalem is a prime example of this.

- **Aid to Christian Civilians**: In several instances, Salah ad-Din personally intervened to provide assistance to Christian civilians caught in the crossfire of the Crusades. On multiple occasions, he ensured that Christian pilgrims were allowed to safely travel to Jerusalem, even during times of war. His respect for civilian life, regardless of religion, earned him the admiration of both his contemporaries and later historians.

A Legacy of Compassion in Warfare

SALAH AD-DIN'S COMPASSION and mercy became central to his legacy, distinguishing him from many other military leaders of his time. His actions helped redefine what it meant to be a just and honorable warrior, and his reputation as a merciful conqueror spread throughout both the Islamic and Christian worlds. His balanced approach to war—combining strength and decisiveness with mercy and restraint—has continued to influence ideas of ethical leadership and just warfare.

- **Admiration from Enemies**: Salah ad-Din's chivalrous behavior did not go unnoticed by his enemies. Richard the Lionheart, his chief adversary during the Third Crusade, reportedly held him in high regard, and the two leaders developed a mutual respect despite their opposing roles in the conflict. In later European literature, Salah ad-Din was often portrayed as the ideal noble adversary—valiant in battle but compassionate in victory.

- **Mercy as a Strategic Tool**: While his compassion was rooted in genuine ethical beliefs, Salah ad-Din also understood the strategic value of mercy. By treating prisoners and civilians with fairness, he minimized resistance from conquered populations and earned the loyalty of many former enemies. His willingness to show mercy also helped foster alliances and maintain stability in the regions he ruled.

Conclusion: The Power of Compassion in Leadership

SALAH AD-DIN'S ABILITY to balance strength with compassion offers valuable lessons for modern leaders. His example shows that true strength is not demonstrated by ruthlessness or cruelty, but by the ability to act with humanity and mercy even in the face of conflict. In a world that often values power and dominance, Salah ad-Din's legacy reminds us that compassion and justice are not signs of weakness, but of moral strength.

By showing mercy toward prisoners and adversaries, Salah ad-Din created a lasting legacy of ethical leadership. His actions demonstrate that leaders who lead with compassion, even in difficult times, can inspire loyalty, build stronger communities, and leave behind a legacy that endures far beyond their time.

Lesson for Today: Compassion as a Key Component of Effective Leadership

IN MODERN LEADERSHIP, compassion is often overlooked in favor of strength, authority, or efficiency. Yet, as Salah ad-Din's life exemplifies, true leadership requires balancing strength with kindness. Compassion is not a sign of weakness but a powerful tool for gaining loyalty, fostering trust, and ensuring long-term success. Today's leaders can learn from Salah ad-Din's approach to leadership, which combined decisiveness and military prowess with empathy and mercy, showing that a leader's humanity can be their greatest asset.

1. Leading with Empathy and Understanding

HISTORICAL INSIGHT: Salah ad-Din's treatment of prisoners, civilians, and even his enemies during the Crusades demonstrated his deep empathy and understanding of others. His ability to place himself in the shoes of those suffering from war, and his actions to alleviate their pain, won him the admiration of both his followers and his foes.

Modern Application: Leaders today can cultivate empathy by actively listening to their teams, understanding their struggles, and taking steps to address their needs. Empathy allows leaders to connect with their employees on a deeper level, fostering a sense of trust and loyalty that goes beyond traditional authority. It's about more than just solving problems; it's about showing a genuine interest in the well-being of others.

- **Example**: A manager who takes time to understand the personal and professional challenges faced by their employees—whether it's balancing work and family or navigating career growth—can offer meaningful support. This might include flexible work hours, mental health resources, or simply providing a listening ear, demonstrating that they care about their employees as people, not just workers.

---

2. Balancing Strength with Kindness

HISTORICAL INSIGHT: Despite being a formidable warrior, Salah ad-Din was known for his acts of kindness, even toward his enemies. His decision to show mercy to the Christian inhabitants of Jerusalem, allowing them to leave the city unharmed, showcased his ability to balance strength in battle with kindness in victory. His compassion did not diminish his authority; instead, it enhanced his reputation as a just and honorable leader.

Modern Application: Leaders today can be both strong and kind. Strength in leadership comes from being decisive, maintaining high standards, and holding people accountable, but it should always be tempered with kindness and understanding. Leaders who balance these traits are more likely to inspire long-term loyalty and respect, rather than fear or resentment.

- **Example**: In a corporate setting, a leader might enforce high performance standards but do so with empathy. When an employee underperforms, instead of reprimanding them harshly, the leader could approach the situation with understanding—perhaps the employee is dealing with personal issues or lacks resources. Offering support while maintaining expectations creates a culture of both accountability and compassion.

3. Gaining Loyalty Through Humanity

HISTORICAL INSIGHT: Salah ad-Din earned the loyalty of his soldiers, subjects, and even former adversaries through his humanity. His willingness to share in the hardships of war and to treat his enemies with mercy made him a leader people were willing to follow out of respect, not fear. His reputation as a compassionate leader extended even beyond the Muslim world, earning him admiration from his Christian rivals, including Richard the Lionheart.

Modern Application: Loyalty is not built through fear or rigid control but through trust, fairness, and demonstrating that you care about the well-being of those you lead. Leaders who show vulnerability and act with humanity foster a deep sense of loyalty that cannot be manufactured through authority alone.

- **Example**: A CEO who makes a point to know their employees, recognize their contributions, and celebrate their successes will inspire a more loyal workforce than one who remains distant and disconnected. By showing that they care about their employees as individuals, leaders can cultivate a sense of belonging that motivates people to go the extra mile.

---

4. Compassion in Conflict Resolution

HISTORICAL INSIGHT: Salah ad-Din's ability to show mercy, even in moments of conflict, demonstrated the power of compassion in resolving disputes. Instead of seeking revenge or retaliation, he often sought peaceful resolutions that spared lives and minimized suffering. His decision to ransom Crusader prisoners rather than execute them, and to allow the peaceful exit of civilians from Jerusalem, showed his preference for resolving conflict with minimal harm.

Modern Application: Compassion is essential in conflict resolution, whether in the workplace, within communities, or in international relations. Leaders who approach conflict with empathy and a desire for reconciliation, rather than punishment, are more likely to create lasting solutions that build stronger relationships rather than deepening divides.

- **Example**: In a team setting, when conflicts arise between employees, a compassionate leader would focus on understanding both sides, mediating with empathy, and finding a solution that satisfies all parties. This approach not only resolves the immediate issue but also builds trust and respect among team members.

---

5. Building a Culture of Compassion

HISTORICAL INSIGHT: Salah ad-Din's compassion extended beyond individual acts; it was a guiding principle in his leadership. By setting an example of kindness and mercy, he fostered a culture of respect and humanity among his followers. His generals and soldiers often emulated his behavior, showing mercy and fairness in their dealings with others.

Modern Application: Compassionate leadership sets the tone for an entire organization. When leaders consistently act with kindness and empathy, they create a culture where employees feel valued and respected. This type of environment encourages collaboration, innovation, and loyalty, as people are more likely to give their best when they feel genuinely cared for.

- **Example**: A company that prioritizes compassion in its leadership—through policies that support work-life balance, mental health, and employee development—will attract and retain top talent. Employees in such a culture are more likely to stay engaged and committed to the company's success.

---

6. Compassion as a Strategic Leadership Tool

HISTORICAL INSIGHT: Salah ad-Din's acts of compassion were not just rooted in ethical beliefs; they also had strategic value. His mercy toward prisoners and conquered populations helped minimize resistance and fostered goodwill, even among former enemies. By showing that he could be both a strong leader and a compassionate one, he was able to maintain stability and loyalty in the regions he ruled.

Modern Application: In today's complex and competitive environments, compassion can be a strategic tool for leaders. It helps to build stronger relationships, reduce conflict, and create a more cohesive team. Leaders who are seen as fair, kind, and empathetic are more likely to inspire collaboration and innovation, as their teams feel safe to express ideas and take risks.

- **Example**: In negotiations, a leader who approaches the opposing party with empathy—understanding their needs and concerns—will often achieve better results than one who takes an adversarial stance. Compassion can lead to more effective partnerships and stronger long-term alliances.

Conclusion: The Strength of Compassionate Leadership

SALAH AD-DIN'S LEGACY teaches us that compassion is not a weakness but a form of strength. Leaders who balance strength with kindness, who show empathy even in moments of conflict, and who act with humanity and fairness, earn the trust and loyalty of those they lead. In today's world, where leadership is often associated with authority and control, the power of compassionate leadership offers a more sustainable and effective path to success.

By leading with empathy, balancing strength with kindness, and demonstrating humanity in every interaction, modern leaders can create environments of trust, collaboration, and loyalty. Compassion isn't just a moral virtue; it's a key component of leadership that inspires people to give their best, even in the most challenging times.

Part II: The Strategy of a Sultan

Chapter 4: Strategic Patience

Historical Insight: Salah ad-Din's Strategic Patience and the Victory at Hattin

Salah ad-Din's success as a military leader was not solely due to his battlefield prowess or the strength of his armies. One of his most crucial assets was his ability to exercise strategic patience. Rather than rushing into battles without adequate preparation, he often waited for the most opportune moment to strike, consolidating his forces, gathering resources, and carefully planning his campaigns. This patient approach allowed him to maximize his chances of success and avoid unnecessary losses.

A prime example of Salah ad-Din's strategic patience was his victory at the Battle of Hattin in 1187, a decisive confrontation between his forces and the Crusaders that paved the way for the recapture of Jerusalem. His careful, methodical planning in the months leading up to this battle showcases the importance of timing and preparation in achieving military and political objectives.

The Prelude to Hattin: Consolidating Power and Gathering Resources

CONSOLIDATING POWER: Before launching his full-scale campaign against the Crusader states, Salah ad-Din spent years consolidating his power base across Egypt, Syria, and other regions under Muslim control. His goal was to unite the Muslim world under his leadership, ensuring that his forces were cohesive, well-equipped, and ready for the challenges ahead. Salah ad-Din understood that without unity and a strong foundation, any campaign against the Crusaders would be fraught with risk.

- **Diplomatic Alliances and Military Preparations**: Salah ad-Din spent years forging alliances with neighboring Muslim leaders, ensuring that when the time came to strike, he could call on a broad coalition of forces. His diplomatic efforts were critical to his success, as they prevented internal conflicts and allowed him to focus on the Crusaders. He also ensured that his armies were well-prepared by reorganizing military structures, replenishing supplies, and improving logistical capabilities.

Avoiding Premature Engagements: While smaller skirmishes and raids occurred between Muslim and Crusader forces, Salah ad-Din avoided major confrontations with the Crusaders until he was certain that the conditions were in his favor. Rather than engaging in costly battles with uncertain outcomes, he focused on weakening the Crusaders over time by targeting their resources, laying siege to isolated fortresses, and cutting off supply lines. This approach wore down the Crusader forces and made them more vulnerable when the time came for a decisive battle.

The Battle of Hattin: Striking at the Right Moment

THE SITUATION IN 1187: By the summer of 1187, Salah ad-Din had sufficiently weakened the Crusader states through years of attrition and strategic positioning. The Crusaders were struggling with internal divisions, a shortage of resources, and the effects of constant harassment by Muslim forces. Salah ad-Din recognized that the time was finally right for a full-scale assault.

Luring the Crusaders into Vulnerability: Salah ad-Din's strategic patience culminated in his decision to lure the Crusader army into a vulnerable position at the Horns of Hattin, a dry and barren region near the Sea of Galilee. By cutting off their access to water and positioning his forces in advantageous terrain, he ensured that the Crusader army would be at a severe disadvantage before the battle even began.

- **Exploiting the Crusaders' Desperation**: Salah ad-Din's strategy worked brilliantly. The Crusaders, desperate to relieve the besieged city of Tiberias and confident that their knights could defeat the Muslim forces in open battle, marched into the arid plains of Hattin without proper access to water. Weakened by thirst and exhaustion, they were no match for Salah ad-Din's well-prepared and strategically positioned army.

The Battle Itself: On July 4, 1187, Salah ad-Din's forces decisively defeated the Crusader army. His careful preparation, combined with his exploitation of the Crusaders' weaknesses, led to one of the most important victories in medieval history. The bulk of the Crusader forces were either killed or captured, including King Guy of Lusignan, the king of Jerusalem. This victory not only crushed the Crusaders' military power but also opened the path for Salah ad-Din to recapture Jerusalem just a few months later.

The Importance of Timing in Salah ad-Din's Strategy

SALAH AD-DIN'S VICTORY at Hattin demonstrates his keen understanding of the importance of timing in military strategy. By exercising patience and waiting for the right moment to strike, he was able to achieve a decisive victory with minimal losses. His ability to assess the broader situation—both his own forces and the weaknesses of his enemies—was critical in ensuring that when he did engage in battle, the odds were overwhelmingly in his favor.

Avoiding Recklessness: Throughout his campaigns, Salah ad-Din was careful to avoid reckless actions that could have jeopardized his long-term goals. He understood that rushing into battle, even when victory seemed likely, could lead to unnecessary casualties or setbacks. Instead, he focused on controlling the pace of the conflict, engaging only when he had maximized his chances of success.

- **Building Long-Term Strength**: Salah ad-Din's strategic patience extended beyond individual battles. He was always thinking about the long-term strength of his forces, ensuring that they were well-supplied and unified. By carefully planning his campaigns and avoiding unnecessary risks, he preserved the strength of his armies for the most critical moments, such as Hattin and the subsequent recapture of Jerusalem.

The Broader Impact of Strategic Patience

SALAH AD-DIN'S STRATEGIC patience had a lasting impact on the Crusader states and the broader conflict between the Muslim and Christian worlds. His victory at Hattin shattered the myth of Crusader invincibility and significantly weakened their presence in the Holy Land. Moreover, his patient approach to warfare allowed him to conserve his resources and maintain the loyalty of his allies, ensuring that his campaigns would be sustainable over the long term.

A Model for Future Leaders: Salah ad-Din's approach to strategy—balancing preparation, patience, and decisive action—served as a model for future military leaders. His ability to bide his time and wait for the right moment to strike is a lesson in the value of strategic foresight and restraint. By not rushing into battle and instead carefully planning his moves, Salah ad-Din was able to achieve lasting success and secure his place in history as one of the greatest military leaders of his time.

Conclusion: The Power of Strategic Patience

SALAH AD-DIN'S VICTORY at Hattin is a testament to the power of strategic patience. Rather than acting impulsively or seeking quick victories, he took the time to build his strength, weaken his enemies, and wait for the ideal moment to strike. His ability to think long-term and avoid unnecessary risks allowed him to achieve a decisive victory that shaped the course of history.

Leaders today can learn from Salah ad-Din's example. Whether in military, business, or personal endeavors, strategic patience is often the key to success. By taking the time to prepare, assess the situation, and strike only when the conditions are favorable, leaders can maximize their chances of achieving their goals while minimizing risks. Salah ad-Din's legacy reminds us that in leadership, as in warfare, timing is everything.

Lesson for Today: The Importance of Patience and Timing in Decision-Making

IN TODAY'S FAST-PACED world, the pressure to act quickly can often lead to hasty decisions and missed opportunities. Salah ad-Din's strategic patience, particularly in the lead-up to the Battle of Hattin, offers a powerful lesson for modern leaders and decision-makers. His ability to wait for the right moment, carefully assess the situation, and avoid impulsive choices allowed him to secure a decisive victory with long-term benefits. This chapter will explore how strategic patience can be applied in business, personal endeavors, and leadership, emphasizing the value of timing in making effective decisions.

1. Patience in Business: Building Long-Term Success

HISTORICAL INSIGHT: Salah ad-Din's refusal to engage in premature battles with the Crusaders, despite having opportunities, illustrates his understanding that patience is essential to achieving sustainable success. He focused on long-term goals, such as uniting the Muslim world and ensuring his forces were strong and prepared, rather than pursuing short-term victories that could have weakened his position.

Modern Application: In business, leaders often face pressure to act quickly—whether it's launching a product, making an investment, or responding to competitors. However, acting too soon without thorough preparation can lead to missed opportunities or failures. Strategic patience involves taking the time to gather information, build the necessary resources, and ensure that all factors are aligned before making a major move.

- **Example**: A startup company might feel pressure to launch a product quickly to beat competitors to market.

However, by taking the time to perfect the product, gather customer feedback, and ensure operational readiness, the company is more likely to have a successful launch that leads to long-term growth rather than a rushed, short-lived success.

Avoiding Impulsive Decisions: Business leaders should avoid making decisions based on immediate pressure or short-term trends. By stepping back and considering the broader context—such as market conditions, customer needs, and long-term strategy—leaders can make more informed and impactful choices. Salah ad-Din's strategic patience reminds us that waiting for the right moment often yields better results than acting hastily.

- **Example**: A CEO considering an acquisition might feel pressure from stakeholders to act quickly. However, by taking the time to assess the financials, cultural fit, and long-term implications of the acquisition, the CEO can avoid costly mistakes and ensure that the decision supports the company's long-term strategy.

---

2. Personal Endeavors: Achieving Goals with Patience

HISTORICAL INSIGHT: Salah ad-Din's methodical approach to his campaigns, where he often waited years to achieve his ultimate goal of recapturing Jerusalem, highlights the importance of patience in pursuing long-term objectives. He understood that rushing could lead to setbacks, but careful planning and patience would ensure lasting success.

Modern Application: In personal endeavors, whether it's career advancement, education, or personal growth, patience is often the key to achieving meaningful success. The desire for immediate results can lead to frustration or burnout, but adopting a long-term perspective allows for steady progress and deeper fulfillment.

- **Example**: A professional seeking to advance in their career might feel frustrated by slow progress. However, by focusing on continuous learning, networking, and building skills over time, they are more likely to achieve a lasting and fulfilling career trajectory. Patience allows them to wait for the right opportunities instead of rushing into roles that may not be the best fit.

Waiting for the Right Opportunities: Like Salah ad-Din, who carefully chose the right moments to engage in battle, individuals should wait for opportunities that align with their long-term goals rather than pursuing every available option. This requires the discipline to say no to short-term gains in favor of long-term success.

- **Example**: A writer might receive offers for projects that don't align with their personal or professional goals. Instead of taking every opportunity, they can wait for the right project that matches their vision, ensuring that their work reflects their values and contributes to their long-term goals.

3. Leadership Decisions: Strategic Patience in Guiding Teams

HISTORICAL INSIGHT: Salah ad-Din's ability to exercise patience in his leadership decisions, such as avoiding major confrontations with the Crusaders until he had maximized his chances of success, demonstrates the importance of waiting for the right moment. By allowing his forces to grow stronger and his enemies weaker, he ensured that when he did engage in battle, he was in the best possible position to succeed.

Modern Application: Leaders today face similar challenges, particularly in guiding their teams or organizations through complex situations. Acting too quickly, without proper preparation or assessment, can lead to poor decisions that negatively impact the organization. Strategic patience involves taking the time to gather information, consult with key stakeholders, and consider the long-term consequences of decisions before taking action.

- **Example**: A company undergoing a major reorganization might be tempted to implement changes rapidly to meet deadlines or external expectations. However, by taking the time to engage employees, gather input, and plan the transition carefully, the leadership can ensure a smoother and more successful transformation.

Making Informed Decisions: Patience in leadership allows for more informed decision-making. By resisting the pressure to act immediately and instead waiting for all the necessary information, leaders can make decisions that are more likely to lead to successful outcomes.

- **Example**: A manager considering the promotion of an employee might wait to observe the employee's performance over time, gather feedback from peers, and assess how the promotion aligns with the team's overall goals. This measured approach ensures that the promotion is based on merit and long-term fit rather than immediate pressures or assumptions.

4. Timing as a Key to Success

HISTORICAL INSIGHT: Salah ad-Din's victory at the Battle of Hattin is a perfect example of how timing can make all the difference. By waiting until the Crusaders were at their most vulnerable—thirsty, tired, and poorly positioned—he was able to win a decisive victory with minimal losses. His ability to assess the situation and strike at the right moment ensured that his actions had maximum impact.

Modern Application: Timing is often a critical factor in decision-making, whether in business, leadership, or personal life. Acting too soon can lead to missed opportunities or failure, while acting too late may mean losing out to competitors or other challenges. Strategic patience involves recognizing when the conditions are right to take action and having the discipline to wait until that moment arrives.

- **Example**: A company launching a new product might choose to wait until market conditions are more favorable, such as during a period of increased consumer demand or when competitors are less active. By waiting for the right timing, the company can maximize the impact of the product launch and achieve better results.

Avoiding Rushed Decisions: In many cases, the pressure to act quickly can lead to rushed decisions that don't consider all the variables. By exercising patience and carefully evaluating the situation, leaders can ensure that their actions are well-timed and well-executed, leading to more successful outcomes.

- **Example**: A team leader facing a challenging project deadline might resist the urge to rush the planning process. Instead, they could invest time in ensuring that the team has the resources, skills, and support needed to complete the project efficiently and effectively. This approach ensures higher-quality work and a better outcome in the long run.

---

5. The Long-Term Benefits of Patience

HISTORICAL INSIGHT: Salah ad-Din's strategic patience allowed him to achieve long-term success rather than focusing on short-term gains. His methodical approach, whether in uniting the Muslim world or planning his campaigns, ensured that his victories were sustainable and had lasting impact.

Modern Application: In any field, the ability to exercise patience often leads to more sustainable success. Quick wins may offer immediate gratification, but long-term success requires careful planning, consistent effort, and the discipline to wait for the right opportunities.

- **Example**: An investor might choose to wait for the right market conditions to make an investment, focusing on long-term growth rather than short-term fluctuations. By being patient and strategic, they can achieve better returns and minimize risk.

Building Long-Term Relationships: Patience is also essential in building strong, lasting relationships, whether in business or personal life. Rushing into partnerships or decisions can lead to misunderstandings and conflicts, but taking the time to build trust and ensure mutual alignment leads to stronger and more enduring relationships.

- **Example**: In negotiating a business deal, a leader might choose to take time to understand the needs and concerns of the other party, building a foundation of trust. This patient approach often leads to stronger partnerships and better outcomes for both sides.

Conclusion: Strategic Patience as a Path to Success

SALAH AD-DIN'S EXAMPLE of strategic patience teaches us that success is not always about acting quickly, but about acting wisely. By waiting for the right moment, gathering the necessary resources, and carefully assessing the situation, leaders can make decisions that are more likely to lead to long-term success. Whether in business, personal growth, or leadership, patience and timing are crucial components of effective decision-making.

In a world that often prioritizes speed, Salah ad-Din's legacy reminds us that sometimes the best course of action is to wait, plan, and prepare. Strategic patience is a powerful tool for achieving lasting success and avoiding the pitfalls of impulsive decisions.

Chapter 5: Adaptability in Battle

Historical Insight: Salah ad-Din's Tactical Adaptability

Salah ad-Din's military success was not only due to his strategic patience but also to his remarkable ability to adapt his tactics to the changing conditions of the battlefield. Whether facing larger Crusader forces in open battle or engaging in smaller, more agile skirmishes, he mastered the art of adjusting his approach based on the terrain, resources, and strengths of his army. This adaptability allowed him to outmaneuver his opponents and achieve victories in situations where traditional methods might have failed.

Salah ad-Din's ability to switch between guerrilla tactics and conventional warfare, depending on the circumstances, was a key factor in his long-term success. His flexible and dynamic approach to warfare ensured that his forces were always able to exploit their advantages, even when facing challenges like unfamiliar terrain or superior Crusader technology.

Adapting to the Terrain and Conditions

USING THE TERRAIN TO His Advantage: Salah ad-Din understood that terrain played a crucial role in the outcome of battles. He carefully chose his battlefields, often positioning his forces in ways that maximized their mobility and minimized the advantages of the heavily armored Crusaders. Whether it was mountainous terrain, deserts, or narrow passes, he always adapted his tactics to fit the environment.

- **Example: The Battle of Hattin (1187)**: The battle was fought on arid, dry plains near the Horns of Hattin. Salah ad-Din exploited the terrain by cutting off the Crusaders' access to water, weakening them before the battle even began. By positioning his forces in advantageous locations, he ensured that the Crusaders, already fatigued from the heat and lack of water, would be fighting uphill against a well-prepared Muslim army. The terrain was a decisive factor in this victory, and Salah ad-Din's understanding of it allowed him to achieve overwhelming success.

Adaptation to Desert Warfare: Salah ad-Din's ability to adapt to the harsh desert environment of the Middle East was another example of his tactical flexibility. He trained his forces to be highly mobile, using lighter armor and faster horses than the Crusaders. This gave his troops an advantage in desert skirmishes, where mobility and endurance were key.

- **Example: Desert Skirmishes with Crusader Forces**: In the deserts of Palestine and Egypt, Salah ad-Din often used hit-and-run tactics against Crusader forces. His lightly armored cavalry could strike quickly and retreat before the heavily armored Crusaders could respond. These guerrilla tactics not only wore down the Crusaders but also allowed Salah ad-Din to conserve his forces for larger battles. His ability to adapt to the unique demands of desert warfare gave him a distinct edge over his enemies.

Using Guerrilla Tactics When Necessary

THE POWER OF GUERRILLA Warfare: Salah ad-Din did not always engage his enemies in large, set-piece battles. When faced with a superior force or unfavorable conditions, he used guerrilla tactics to harass and weaken his enemies over time. These tactics, which included hit-and-run attacks, ambushes, and raids on supply lines, allowed him to undermine the Crusaders without committing to risky large-scale confrontations.

- **Example: Raids on Crusader Supply Lines**: Throughout his campaigns, Salah ad-Din often focused on cutting off Crusader supply lines, forcing them into positions of weakness. By harassing the Crusaders' caravans and disrupting their flow of resources, he effectively weakened their ability to fight. These raids were especially useful when he needed to delay the Crusaders or prevent them from regrouping after a defeat. Guerrilla tactics allowed him to keep the Crusaders off balance and constantly on the defensive.

Using Mobility to His Advantage: The strength of Salah ad-Din's forces lay in their mobility and ability to strike quickly. His army, particularly his cavalry, was highly trained in fast, agile maneuvers. This allowed him to execute hit-and-run tactics that kept his enemies on edge and made it difficult for the slower, heavier Crusader forces to respond effectively.

- **Example: The Siege of Acre (1189–1191)**: During the lengthy Siege of Acre, Salah ad-Din's forces used guerrilla tactics to disrupt the Crusaders' supply lines and reinforcements. While unable to break the siege, his strategy significantly slowed the Crusaders' advance and forced them to fight on his terms. These smaller-scale, targeted attacks weakened the Crusader forces and prevented them from fully consolidating their power in the region.

Shifting to Conventional Warfare When Needed

ADAPTING TO LARGE-SCALE Warfare: While Salah ad-Din was highly skilled in guerrilla warfare, he was also adept at leading large, conventional battles when the situation called for it. When the time came for decisive engagements, such as the Battle of Hattin or the Siege of Jerusalem, he was able to marshal his forces and execute complex battlefield strategies. His flexibility in shifting between small-scale and large-scale warfare made him a formidable opponent.

- **Example: The Recapture of Jerusalem (1187)**: After his victory at Hattin, Salah ad-Din turned his attention to the recapture of Jerusalem, one of the most significant objectives of his military career. This was not a guerrilla engagement but a well-planned, large-scale siege operation. Salah ad-Din's forces systematically encircled the city, cutting off its supplies and forcing the Crusader defenders to surrender. His ability to lead both smaller, agile forces and large-scale conventional armies allowed him to adapt to different types of warfare and succeed in both.

Coordinating Large-Scale Operations: Salah ad-Din's military success also came from his ability to coordinate large-scale military campaigns across multiple fronts. He maintained communication and logistical support for his forces, ensuring that his armies were well-supplied and able to operate effectively in a variety of conditions.

- **Example: The Coordination of Forces During the Third Crusade (1189–1192)**: During the Third Crusade, Salah ad-Din faced a renewed offensive from European forces led by King Richard the Lionheart. Salah ad-Din adapted his tactics to the Crusaders' conventional warfare, defending key cities while employing guerrilla tactics to delay their progress. His ability to shift between different forms of warfare helped him hold off the Crusader advance and preserve Muslim control over Jerusalem and other key territories.

Flexibility as a Core Leadership Trait

SALAH AD-DIN'S ADAPTABILITY was not just a military skill—it was a core aspect of his leadership philosophy. He understood that no single approach would work in every situation and that success depended on the ability to adapt to changing circumstances. This flexibility extended beyond the battlefield to his diplomatic and governance strategies, where he often adjusted his tactics to suit the political and social realities of the moment.

- **Diplomatic Adaptability**: In addition to his military flexibility, Salah ad-Din was also a skilled diplomat who adapted his strategies to build alliances, negotiate with rivals, and maintain the loyalty of his supporters. His ability to balance military action with diplomacy allowed him to maintain a unified Muslim front while keeping the Crusaders at bay.

- **Example: Negotiations with Richard the Lionheart**: During the Third Crusade, Salah ad-Din engaged in negotiations with Richard the Lionheart, even as they fought on the battlefield. He understood that diplomacy could achieve what military force could not, and by maintaining open lines of communication with Richard, he was able to preserve Muslim control over Jerusalem while avoiding unnecessary bloodshed.

Conclusion: Adaptability as a Key to Success

SALAH AD-DIN'S SUCCESS as a leader and military commander was rooted in his ability to adapt to changing conditions. Whether it was adjusting his tactics to fit the terrain, employing guerrilla warfare to wear down his enemies, or shifting to large-scale conventional battles when necessary, he always remained flexible and open to new approaches. This adaptability allowed him to outmaneuver his opponents and achieve his long-term goals.

Modern leaders can learn from Salah ad-Din's example. In today's rapidly changing world, the ability to adapt to new challenges, seize opportunities, and adjust strategies based on the situation is more important than ever. Whether in business, leadership, or personal endeavors, adaptability is a crucial trait for success. By staying flexible and ready to adjust, leaders can navigate complex environments and achieve their goals, just as Salah ad-Din did centuries ago.

Lesson for Today: The Importance of Adaptability in a Rapidly Changing World

IN TODAY'S DYNAMIC and fast-paced world, the ability to adapt is essential for success. Whether in leadership, business, or personal life, those who remain flexible in the face of challenges, pivot strategies when needed, and stay open to new solutions are the ones who thrive. Salah ad-Din's mastery of adaptability—both in battle and in his broader leadership decisions—provides a timeless lesson for modern leaders and individuals on how to navigate uncertainty and complexity with confidence.

1. Flexibility in the Face of Challenges

HISTORICAL INSIGHT: Salah ad-Din's success in warfare was largely due to his ability to adapt his tactics based on the terrain, the strength of his forces, and the resources at his disposal. He didn't rely on a single approach; instead, he assessed each situation and adjusted his strategies accordingly. His willingness to change tactics—whether employing guerrilla warfare or large-scale operations—allowed him to overcome challenges that might have defeated a less adaptable leader.

Modern Application: In today's world, leaders and individuals face constantly shifting challenges, whether due to technological advancements, economic fluctuations, or changing social dynamics. Flexibility is critical to overcoming these challenges. Leaders who are rigid in their approach may struggle when circumstances change, but those who can pivot and adjust their strategies are better equipped to find success.

- **Example**: A company facing a sudden shift in market demand might need to pivot its business model or product offerings. Instead of stubbornly sticking to a strategy that no longer works, a flexible leader would be open to exploring new markets, adjusting products, or even changing the business structure to meet evolving customer needs.

Adapt to Changing Environments: The ability to adjust to different environments—be they external market conditions, team dynamics, or unexpected obstacles—is a key aspect of adaptability. Leaders should constantly scan their environment for signs of change and be prepared to modify their approach to better fit the new reality.

- **Example**: A manager overseeing a project may encounter unforeseen setbacks such as resource shortages or changes in client expectations. Instead of pushing forward with the original plan, a flexible manager would reassess the situation, make necessary adjustments, and reallocate resources to ensure the project's success in its new context.

---

2. Learning to Pivot Strategies

HISTORICAL INSIGHT: Salah ad-Din's ability to pivot his strategies was evident throughout his campaigns. When faced with stronger or better-equipped Crusader forces, he didn't engage them directly in traditional combat. Instead, he used guerrilla tactics, cutting off their supply lines and weakening them over time. When the situation changed, he adapted again, leading his forces in conventional warfare during major battles like the Battle of Hattin. His ability to shift between strategies ensured his victories and helped him achieve long-term success.

Modern Application: Pivoting strategies is often necessary in business, leadership, and personal life. When initial plans don't work, or when new information comes to light, successful leaders are those who can change course without hesitation. This doesn't mean abandoning long-term goals but finding new paths to reach them.

- **Example**: A startup founder might begin with a specific product idea that doesn't gain traction in the market. Instead of giving up, a flexible founder would pivot by listening to customer feedback and refining the product or even shifting to an entirely new idea that better aligns with market demands.

Embrace Failure as Feedback: One of the key aspects of adaptability is learning to view setbacks and failures as valuable feedback. Instead of seeing a failed strategy as a reason to give up, adaptable leaders treat it as an opportunity to learn, adjust, and pivot to a more effective solution.

- **Example**: A sports coach might implement a game strategy that doesn't work against a particular opponent. Instead of continuing with the same plan, the coach could analyze the game in real-time, make strategic adjustments, and pivot to a different playstyle to outmaneuver the opponent in the next half.

---

3. Staying Open to New Solutions

HISTORICAL INSIGHT: Salah ad-Din's openness to new solutions was key to his adaptability. He wasn't bound by traditional tactics or rigid methods of warfare. Instead, he embraced innovative approaches when necessary, such as using lighter cavalry for faster, more agile movements in desert skirmishes or employing negotiation and diplomacy alongside military action. His ability to stay open to new ideas allowed him to succeed in both military and diplomatic arenas.

Modern Application: In leadership and life, staying open to new solutions is essential for problem-solving and innovation. Leaders who are willing to explore alternative approaches, listen to diverse perspectives, and try new methods are more likely to find effective solutions to complex challenges.

- **Example**: A business facing declining sales might experiment with new marketing strategies, such as adopting social media advertising or partnering with influencers, rather than relying on traditional advertising methods. By being open to new solutions, the company can tap into untapped markets and potentially reverse its sales decline.

Encourage Creativity and Innovation: Leaders who promote a culture of openness to new ideas foster creativity and innovation within their teams. By encouraging team members to propose alternative solutions and challenge conventional thinking, leaders create an environment where adaptability thrives.

- **Example**: A team leader who regularly asks for input from their employees and is open to implementing unconventional solutions creates a workplace where innovation is encouraged. This openness can lead to breakthroughs that would otherwise be missed in a more rigid, top-down decision-making structure.

---

4. Adapting to Unforeseen Circumstances

HISTORICAL INSIGHT: Salah ad-Din's ability to adapt to unforeseen circumstances was critical to his military success. He often found himself facing unexpected challenges, such as Crusader reinforcements or sudden changes in terrain. Yet, his adaptability allowed him to quickly adjust his plans, regroup his forces, and find ways to turn adversity into advantage.

Modern Application: In both leadership and personal life, unforeseen circumstances are inevitable. Whether it's an economic downturn, a technological disruption, or a personal challenge, adaptability means being able to adjust your plans when things don't go as expected. Instead of being thrown off course, adaptable leaders use these situations as opportunities to pivot and move forward with a revised strategy.

- **Example**: A leader in the hospitality industry might face a sudden crisis like the COVID-19 pandemic, which disrupts traditional operations. Rather than accepting defeat, an adaptable leader would quickly pivot to new models, such as offering virtual experiences, delivery services, or flexible cancellation policies, ensuring that the business continues to thrive despite the disruption.

Remain Resilient in the Face of Setbacks: Adaptability is closely tied to resilience. Those who can bounce back from setbacks and find new ways forward are more likely to succeed in the long run. Adaptable leaders don't view obstacles as roadblocks but as opportunities to find new, creative solutions.

- **Example**: A personal goal, such as completing a marathon, might be interrupted by an injury. Instead of giving up, an adaptable individual would adjust their training plan, perhaps focusing on recovery or switching to a different form of exercise, ensuring that they remain active and focused on long-term fitness goals.

5. The Long-Term Benefits of Adaptability

HISTORICAL INSIGHT: Salah ad-Din's adaptability contributed to his long-term success as both a military leader and a statesman. His ability to adjust his tactics based on circumstances ensured that he could achieve his broader goals, such as uniting the Muslim world and recapturing Jerusalem. His legacy as a flexible, innovative leader remains an example of how adaptability leads to lasting impact.

Modern Application: In leadership, business, and personal life, those who remain adaptable are more likely to achieve lasting success. The ability to pivot, embrace new solutions, and adjust to changing environments ensures that individuals and organizations remain competitive and relevant in a constantly evolving world.

- **Example**: A tech company that constantly adapts to new technological advancements and market trends will remain innovative and successful, while a company that sticks to outdated methods may fall behind its competitors. Flexibility is key to staying relevant in rapidly changing industries.

Fostering Continuous Growth: Adaptability is not just about responding to change; it's about anticipating it and continuously evolving. Leaders who build adaptability into their approach to life and work foster a mindset of growth and development, always looking for ways to improve and stay ahead of the curve.

- **Example**: A lifelong learner who regularly updates their skills, learns new technologies, and embraces change will remain relevant and successful in their career, even as industries evolve and new challenges arise.

Conclusion: Adaptability as a Core Leadership Skill

SALAH AD-DIN'S ABILITY to adapt his tactics, strategies, and approaches to different situations serves as a powerful reminder of the importance of adaptability in leadership and life. In a rapidly changing world, the ability to stay flexible, pivot strategies, and remain open to new solutions is essential for long-term success.

Modern leaders and individuals who embrace adaptability are better equipped to navigate uncertainty, overcome challenges, and seize opportunities. By learning to adjust to new realities, pivot when necessary, and remain open to creative solutions, we can achieve our goals and thrive in an ever-changing world. Just as Salah ad-Din's adaptability enabled him to achieve lasting success, our own flexibility and willingness to evolve will be key to our success in the future.

Chapter 6: Defending with Honor

Historical Insight: Salah ad-Din's Ethical Approach to Warfare and the Defense of Jerusalem

Salah ad-Din's defense of Jerusalem not only demonstrated his military expertise but also highlighted his deep commitment to ethical warfare. In an era marked by brutal conquests and widespread violence, his actions during and after the siege of Jerusalem in 1187 stand out as an example of leadership with integrity, compassion, and restraint. Rather than exacting vengeance on the city or its inhabitants, he took great care to ensure the preservation of Jerusalem and the fair treatment of civilians, regardless of their religion.

The Siege of Jerusalem (1187)

CONTEXT OF THE SIEGE: After the decisive Muslim victory at the Battle of Hattin in July 1187, Salah ad-Din's forces turned their attention to Jerusalem, the ultimate prize in the struggle between Muslim and Crusader forces. By early October 1187, his armies had surrounded the city, and its defense was in the hands of Balian of Ibelin, one of the few remaining Crusader commanders in the region. Many feared a bloody siege and the possibility of a massacre similar to that which occurred during the Crusaders' capture of Jerusalem in 1099.

The Ethical Approach to Siege Warfare: Despite the immense significance of Jerusalem for both Muslims and Christians, Salah ad-Din did not seek to destroy the city or slaughter its inhabitants. Instead, he approached the siege with a sense of responsibility and ethical restraint, determined to avoid the bloodshed that had characterized earlier battles. His military strategy was as much about diplomacy and preserving the city as it was about defeating the Crusader forces.

- **Negotiating Terms of Surrender**: Rather than allowing the siege to drag on and cause unnecessary suffering, Salah ad-Din opened negotiations with Balian of Ibelin. He offered generous terms of surrender, allowing the city's Christian inhabitants to leave safely in exchange for a modest ransom. Those who could not afford the ransom were not abandoned; Salah ad-Din's own brother, Al-Adil, requested that many of the poor be allowed to leave without paying, and Salah ad-Din granted this request.

- **Ensuring Civilian Safety**: Salah ad-Din's humane treatment of the city's civilian population, regardless of their religious affiliation, set him apart from many of the military leaders of his time. He ordered that no harm come to the Christian civilians and that their property and religious sites be respected. The contrast between Salah ad-Din's actions and the brutal sack of Jerusalem by the Crusaders in 1099 was stark, further elevating his reputation as a just and ethical ruler.

Preserving Jerusalem's Religious Sites

RESPECT FOR CHRISTIAN Holy Places: One of Salah ad-Din's key concerns during the defense of Jerusalem was the preservation of the city's religious sites. While the city had immense significance for

Muslims, it was also a sacred place for Christians and Jews. Salah ad-Din took deliberate steps to ensure that Christian holy sites, such as the Church of the Holy Sepulchre, were preserved and that Christian pilgrims would still have access to them. This respect for religious freedom and tolerance was rare during the medieval period, especially in the context of a religiously motivated conflict like the Crusades.

- **No Destruction of Churches**: Unlike the Crusaders, who had desecrated Muslim holy sites during their occupation of Jerusalem, Salah ad-Din made sure that no churches were destroyed or repurposed. Christian clergy were allowed to remain in the city, and Christian pilgrims were permitted to visit their holy sites. This policy of religious tolerance helped to minimize resistance from the city's inhabitants and showed that Salah ad-Din's conquest was not driven by hatred or vengeance but by a desire for justice and peace.

- **Conversion of Al-Aqsa Mosque**: While preserving Christian sites, Salah ad-Din also took steps to restore Muslim control over their holy places. The Al-Aqsa Mosque, which had been converted into a palace by the Crusaders, was returned to its original use as a place of Islamic worship. However, this restoration was carried out with care and respect, without the destruction or looting that often accompanied such changes in control during the Crusades.

Fair Treatment of Captured Soldiers and Leaders

RANSOM INSTEAD OF EXECUTION: After the city's surrender, Salah ad-Din followed the Islamic tradition of offering captured soldiers and leaders the opportunity to be ransomed rather than executed. This act of mercy extended even to the knights and commanders who had fought against him. Unlike many military leaders of his time, who might have sought vengeance through mass executions, Salah ad-Din prioritized justice and mercy, ensuring that captives were treated fairly.

- **Balian of Ibelin's Request**: Balian, who had led the defense of Jerusalem, feared that Salah ad-Din would kill him for his role in the Crusader resistance. However, Salah ad-Din not only spared Balian's life but also allowed him to leave the city honorably, along with his family. This act of mercy demonstrated Salah ad-Din's commitment to ethical conduct in warfare, earning him respect even from his enemies.

Contrast with Crusader Tactics: Salah ad-Din's treatment of captives and civilians stood in stark contrast to the actions of the Crusaders during their capture of Jerusalem in 1099, when they had massacred thousands of Muslims and Jews. By offering generous terms and ensuring the safety of non-combatants, Salah ad-Din set a new standard for ethical conduct in warfare. His decision to prioritize mercy and fairness over revenge cemented his reputation as a noble and honorable leader, admired by both his followers and his foes.

The Broader Ethical Approach to Warfare

A JUST CONQUEROR: Salah ad-Din's defense of Jerusalem, along with his overall conduct during the Crusades, reflects a broader ethical approach to warfare that was deeply rooted in his Islamic faith and personal values. While he was undoubtedly a skilled military leader, his actions showed that he believed in the importance of justice, mercy, and the preservation of life, even in the context of war. This ethical approach extended to his treatment of civilians, his preservation of holy sites, and his willingness to negotiate rather than resort to unnecessary violence.

- **A Moral Victory**: Salah ad-Din's victory in Jerusalem was not just a military triumph; it was a moral one. By defending the city with honor and compassion, he set an example for future generations of leaders on how to conduct warfare with humanity and dignity. His actions demonstrated that it is possible to achieve military success while adhering to ethical principles, even in the heat of battle.

Conclusion: Ethical Leadership in Warfare

SALAH AD-DIN'S DEFENSE of Jerusalem stands as a powerful example of ethical leadership in warfare. While he was a fierce and effective military commander, his actions were guided by a deep sense of justice and compassion. His decision to spare civilians, preserve religious sites, and treat captured enemies with respect showed that true leadership is not just about winning battles, but about conducting oneself with honor and integrity.

Modern leaders can learn from Salah ad-Din's example. Whether in military, political, or business contexts, the ability to lead with both strength and compassion is essential for achieving lasting success. By prioritizing ethics and fairness, leaders can inspire loyalty and respect, even from those who oppose them. Just as Salah ad-Din's legacy endures because of his honorable actions, leaders today can build lasting legacies by leading with justice, mercy, and ethical conduct.

Lesson for Today: Defending Values with Integrity in Leadership

IN ANY LEADERSHIP ROLE, whether in business, politics, or personal life, there will come a time when your values, team, or project will be challenged. How you respond to that challenge can define your success and legacy. Salah ad-Din's ethical approach to defending Jerusalem—where he balanced military prowess with fairness and integrity—offers a timeless lesson for leaders today. Defending one's values and objectives with honor requires firmness in the face of opposition but also fairness and ethical decision-making. By staying true to your principles while leading with compassion and integrity, you can inspire loyalty, build respect, and achieve lasting success.

1. Standing Firm in Defense of Core Values

HISTORICAL INSIGHT: Salah ad-Din's defense of Jerusalem was not just a military effort—it was a defense of his values and his commitment to justice, mercy, and fairness. While many leaders of his time engaged in brutal conquest, Salah ad-Din remained steadfast in his ethical principles, ensuring the safety of civilians and the preservation of holy sites, even in the heat of conflict.

Modern Application: In today's world, defending your values with integrity is crucial, especially when faced with opposition. Whether you are defending a business decision, a team, or a personal belief, standing firm in your core values demonstrates that you are committed to doing what is right, even when it's difficult. This type of ethical leadership builds trust and credibility, showing others that you are willing to fight for what you believe in, but with fairness and respect.

- **Example**: A business leader who values transparency might face pressure to cover up a mistake or mislead stakeholders. Instead of compromising their integrity, the leader could choose to be honest and take responsibility for the error. By defending the value of transparency, the leader builds trust with employees and clients, even in challenging times.

Balancing Firmness with Flexibility: While standing firm in your values is essential, leaders must also recognize when to be flexible in their methods. Like Salah ad-Din, who balanced diplomacy with military strength, effective leaders know when to stand their ground and when to adapt their strategies to meet the needs of the situation.

- **Example**: A project manager might defend the team's overall goals and vision but remain flexible in how those goals are achieved, allowing for adjustments and new ideas that align with the core values of the project.

---

2. Leading with Fairness in the Face of Opposition

HISTORICAL INSIGHT: Salah ad-Din's fairness in victory, particularly his humane treatment of the Christian inhabitants of Jerusalem, demonstrated his commitment to ethical leadership. Rather than seeking revenge or imposing harsh punishments on his defeated enemies, he offered them safe passage and ensured that they were treated with dignity. His fairness in the face of opposition not only preserved the city but also earned him respect from his adversaries.

Modern Application: In leadership, fairness is vital when facing opposition or conflict. Leaders who are fair, even when dealing with competitors or critics, are more likely to build strong relationships and foster long-term success. Fairness doesn't mean weakness—it means treating people with respect, listening to different viewpoints, and making decisions based on justice and ethics, even under pressure.

- **Example**: A company leader involved in a dispute with a competitor might choose to handle the situation with fairness and professionalism, avoiding personal attacks or unethical behavior. This approach preserves the company's reputation and creates a foundation for potential future collaboration or reconciliation.

Ethical Decision-Making in Tough Situations: When faced with difficult decisions, leaders must rely on their ethical compass to guide them. This means evaluating options not just based on what is most expedient, but on what is most fair and just for all involved. Ethical decision-making builds a culture of integrity and trust within the team or organization.

- **Example**: In a leadership role, a manager might be faced with the decision to lay off employees. An ethical approach would involve exploring all options to mitigate the impact, such as offering severance packages or helping with job placement, rather than making decisions solely based on financial gain.

---

3. Building Trust Through Ethical Defense

HISTORICAL INSIGHT: Salah ad-Din's ethical defense of Jerusalem, where he balanced military action with diplomacy and mercy, earned him the trust and admiration of both his allies and enemies. His actions were rooted in a deep sense of justice, and by defending the city with honor and integrity, he built a legacy of trust that extended beyond the battlefield.

Modern Application: In leadership, trust is built not just by achieving success, but by how you achieve it. Defending your values, team, or project with integrity shows others that you are reliable and that your decisions are guided by principles, not self-interest. Trust is one of the most valuable assets a leader can have, and it is earned through consistent ethical behavior, even when under pressure.

- **Example**: A CEO who consistently advocates for ethical business practices, even when it might be easier to cut corners, builds a reputation for integrity. Employees, investors, and customers are more likely to trust a leader who demonstrates a commitment to fairness and ethics, especially in difficult times.

Maintaining Integrity Under Pressure: True integrity is tested when leaders are under pressure. It's easy to act ethically when things are going well, but when faced with conflict or challenges, maintaining your principles becomes more difficult—and more critical. Leaders who stay true to their values in tough situations earn the long-term respect and loyalty of those around them.

- **Example**: A leader facing a high-stakes negotiation might be tempted to engage in manipulative tactics or make false promises. However, by maintaining integrity and negotiating honestly, the leader can build trust with the other party, leading to better outcomes and a stronger reputation.

---

4. Inspiring Others Through Ethical Leadership

HISTORICAL INSIGHT: Salah ad-Din's ethical conduct during the defense of Jerusalem inspired not only his followers but also his adversaries. His ability to combine military strength with fairness and compassion set an example for future leaders and warriors. By defending his people and values with honor, Salah ad-Din became a symbol of ethical leadership that transcended religious and cultural divides.

Modern Application: Leaders who defend their values with integrity inspire others to do the same. By setting an example of ethical leadership, they create a culture where fairness, respect, and justice are prioritized. This type of leadership not only fosters loyalty within a team but also encourages others to adopt similar ethical principles in their own decision-making.

- **Example**: A leader in a nonprofit organization might inspire their team by consistently advocating for the organization's mission, even when faced with financial challenges or external criticism. By staying true to the organization's values, the leader motivates their team to remain dedicated and work toward long-term goals with integrity.

Creating a Culture of Integrity: Ethical leaders set the tone for the entire organization or team. When leaders consistently act with integrity, they inspire others to do the same, creating a culture of trust, respect, and fairness. This culture not only leads to stronger relationships within the team but also enhances the organization's reputation and long-term success.

- **Example**: A business leader who promotes transparency, ethical decision-making, and fairness in all aspects of the company creates a workplace where employees feel valued and empowered to act with integrity in their own roles.

5. The Long-Term Benefits of Ethical Defense

HISTORICAL INSIGHT: Salah ad-Din's ethical approach to warfare and his defense of Jerusalem had lasting benefits. His reputation as a just and honorable leader extended far beyond the Muslim world, earning him the respect of Christian leaders and chroniclers alike. His decision to defend his values with fairness and integrity left a legacy that endured long after his military victories.

Modern Application: Defending your values, team, or project with integrity may not always lead to immediate rewards, but it ensures long-term success and respect. Leaders who prioritize ethics over expediency build strong, lasting relationships with their teams, clients, and stakeholders. Ethical defense leads to sustainable success, while cutting corners or compromising values often results in short-term gains but long-term damage.

- **Example**: A company that prioritizes ethical sourcing and environmental sustainability might face higher costs in the short term, but over time, it builds a loyal customer base and a strong reputation for doing what is right. This ethical defense of values leads to long-term growth and brand loyalty.

Sustaining Ethical Leadership Over Time: Ethical leadership requires consistency. Leaders who defend their values and act with integrity, even when it's difficult, create a strong foundation for long-term success. By making ethical defense a cornerstone of their leadership approach, they build a legacy that endures.

- **Example**: A political leader who advocates for justice and fairness throughout their career, even when facing opposition, may not always win every battle, but they build a legacy of ethical leadership that inspires future generations.

Conclusion: Defending Values with Integrity in Leadership

SALAH AD-DIN'S DEFENSE of Jerusalem stands as a powerful example of how leaders can defend their values, team, or project with honor and integrity. His commitment to fairness, even in the face of opposition, showed that ethical leadership is not about winning at all costs but about achieving success in a way that upholds justice and respect for others.

Modern leaders can learn from Salah ad-Din's approach by staying firm in their values, making fair decisions under pressure, and maintaining integrity in all aspects of their leadership. By defending what matters with honor, leaders build trust, inspire loyalty, and achieve long-term success, creating a lasting legacy of ethical leadership.

Part III: The Ethics of Power

Chapter 7: Leadership Through Justice

Historical Insight: Salah ad-Din's Legacy of Fairness and Justice

Salah ad-Din's reputation as a fair and just ruler was one of the key elements that cemented his legacy, both among his followers and even among his enemies. In a time when power was often maintained through brute force and oppression, Salah ad-Din stood out for his commitment to justice and fairness. He made a concerted effort to ensure that his rule was seen as legitimate, not just through military success but by fostering a system of governance based on equity, mercy, and respect for the law. This approach earned him the loyalty of his subjects, the admiration of his peers, and the grudging respect of his adversaries, including the Christian Crusaders.

Fair Treatment of All Subjects

JUSTICE FOR ALL, REGARDLESS of Faith: One of the defining features of Salah ad-Din's rule was his commitment to fairness, regardless of the religion or background of his subjects. While he was a devout Muslim leader, he ensured that Christians, Jews, and Muslims living under his rule were treated with fairness and had access to justice. Salah ad-Din was known for resolving disputes fairly, protecting the rights of all communities, and maintaining the balance between military leadership and civic responsibility.

- **Example: Treatment of Christian Subjects**: Salah ad-Din's fair treatment of Christian populations in territories he reconquered, such as Jerusalem, was a hallmark of his rule. Unlike previous Crusader leaders, who had massacred or expelled Muslim inhabitants, Salah ad-Din allowed Christians to remain, worship, and even leave peacefully if they wished. His focus on justice over vengeance set him apart and reinforced his image as a just ruler.

- **Fair Governance**: Salah ad-Din appointed local leaders who upheld justice and fairness in governance, ensuring that laws were applied equally and without corruption. His ability to balance strictness with fairness strengthened his rule and kept the regions under his control stable and prosperous.

Respect for the Law: Salah ad-Din did not view himself as above the law. Rather, he respected the principles of Islamic jurisprudence, which emphasized fairness, justice, and mercy. This adherence to legal frameworks earned him the respect of scholars, judges, and ordinary people alike, as they saw him as a ruler who governed by principles rather than personal whims.

A Ruler Respected by His Enemies

ADMIRED BY CHRISTIAN Leaders: Salah ad-Din's reputation for fairness and justice extended far beyond the Muslim world. Christian leaders, including his fiercest adversary, King Richard the Lionheart, came to respect him for his conduct in war and governance. During the Third Crusade, despite being bitter rivals on the battlefield, Salah ad-Din and Richard developed a mutual admiration, with Richard acknowledging Salah ad-Din's fairness in dealing with prisoners and his ethical conduct in negotiations.

- **Example: Treatment of Crusader Prisoners**: After the Battle of Hattin, Salah ad-Din captured a large number of Crusader knights, including King Guy of Lusignan, the king of Jerusalem. Rather than executing them, as many leaders of the time might have done, Salah ad-Din chose to ransom the prisoners and treated them with respect. His sense of justice and mercy, even toward his enemies, earned him the admiration of both his Muslim followers and his Christian rivals.

Diplomacy with Enemies: Salah ad-Din's fairness also extended to his diplomatic efforts. He often sought to negotiate terms that were just and reasonable, even when dealing with defeated foes. His focus on securing peaceful resolutions, when possible, showcased his belief in diplomacy and fairness as tools for sustaining peace, not just military might.

Justice as a Foundation for Legitimacy

BUILDING LEGITIMACY Through Fair Rule: Salah ad-Din's focus on justice and fairness was not just a personal ethic—it was a political strategy that helped solidify his rule. By ensuring that his governance was fair and just, he gained the loyalty and trust of his people, who saw him as a legitimate leader, not just a conqueror. This legitimacy was crucial in maintaining stability across the diverse territories he controlled, from Egypt to Syria.

- **Strengthening Loyalty Among Followers**: Salah ad-Din's fairness in governance helped secure the loyalty of various tribal leaders, local governors, and ordinary citizens.

By creating a system where justice was accessible to all, he fostered a sense of loyalty and unity among his subjects, ensuring that they would support him even in difficult times.

Avoiding Tyranny and Corruption: In an era when many rulers maintained power through fear and corruption, Salah ad-Din's just rule helped him avoid the pitfalls of tyranny. His focus on accountability and his rejection of corruption among his officials created a governance system that was seen as legitimate and trustworthy. This approach not only strengthened his internal control but also attracted allies and strengthened his position in the wider Muslim world.

Balancing Military Might with Mercy

MERCY AS A FORM OF Justice: Salah ad-Din's sense of justice was often tempered by mercy, especially in times of conflict. While he was a skilled and determined military leader, he did not seek unnecessary bloodshed or cruelty. His victories were often marked by acts of mercy, as seen in his treatment of Crusader prisoners, his protection of civilians, and his preservation of holy sites. His combination of military strength and ethical restraint made him both respected and feared by his enemies.

- **Example: The Surrender of Jerusalem (1187)**: When Salah ad-Din recaptured Jerusalem, he could have exacted harsh revenge on the Crusader inhabitants, as the Crusaders had done to Muslims during their initial capture of the city. Instead, he offered the Christians generous terms of surrender, allowing them to leave the city peacefully or remain as residents. This act of mercy was seen as a just and honorable decision, earning him praise from across the medieval world.

Just Warfare: Salah ad-Din's approach to warfare reflected his broader commitment to justice. He avoided unnecessary brutality and emphasized the protection of civilians whenever possible. His belief in just warfare—where military action is carried out with ethical considerations—set him apart from many of his contemporaries and reinforced his reputation as a fair and honorable leader.

Lessons for Modern Leadership: Fairness and Justice as Pillars of Leadership

SALAH AD-DIN'S LEGACY of fairness and justice provides valuable lessons for modern leadership. In a world where power is often associated with dominance and control, his example shows that true leadership is built on fairness, respect for others, and a commitment to justice. Here are key lessons for today's leaders:

1. Fair Treatment Builds Legitimacy

HISTORICAL INSIGHT: Salah ad-Din's fair treatment of his subjects, regardless of their religion or background, helped establish his rule as legitimate in the eyes of his people. His focus on justice, rather than coercion, created a stable and loyal population, which in turn strengthened his authority.

Modern Application: In leadership today, fair treatment of employees, clients, and stakeholders is essential for building long-term legitimacy and trust. Leaders who consistently treat others with fairness—whether in decision-making, conflict resolution, or resource allocation—are more likely to gain the respect and loyalty of their teams. Fairness fosters a sense of belonging and stability, creating a culture where people are motivated to contribute and support the leader's vision.

● **Example**: A CEO who implements transparent, equitable policies for employee promotion and compensation, based on merit rather than favoritism, creates an environment where employees feel valued and are more likely to be loyal and motivated.

---

2. Fairness in Conflict Resolution

HISTORICAL INSIGHT: Salah ad-Din's fair treatment of prisoners and adversaries during the Crusades, especially his willingness to offer reasonable terms of surrender, demonstrated his belief in fairness even in conflict. This earned him the respect of his enemies and helped secure peaceful outcomes that benefited both sides.

Modern Application: Leaders today can learn from Salah ad-Din's example by applying fairness in conflict resolution, whether in negotiations, business disputes, or team conflicts. By focusing on fair and ethical solutions, rather than seeking to dominate or win at all costs, leaders can build stronger relationships and ensure that conflicts are resolved in ways that benefit all parties.

● **Example**: A manager mediating a conflict between team members should listen to both sides fairly, seek to understand the root causes of the conflict, and work toward a solution that respects the perspectives of both individuals, rather than favoring one over the other.

---

3. Justice Strengthens Loyalty and Unity

HISTORICAL INSIGHT: Salah ad-Din's just governance helped unify the diverse populations under his rule. By ensuring that justice was accessible to all, he built a loyal and cohesive population that supported his leadership, even during challenging times.

Modern Application: Justice in leadership fosters unity and loyalty within teams and organizations. When leaders act with fairness, uphold ethical standards, and apply rules consistently, they create a culture of trust and cohesion. This unity helps teams navigate challenges more effectively and strengthens their collective commitment to shared goals.

- **Example**: A leader who holds everyone in the organization to the same standards, regardless of their rank or position, promotes a culture of fairness and accountability. This consistency builds trust and motivates team members to work toward the common good.

Conclusion: Leading with Fairness and Justice

SALAH AD-DIN'S LEGACY as a just and fair leader demonstrates that true power is not just about military or political dominance—it is about ruling with integrity, fairness, and a commitment to justice. His ability to balance strength with compassion, and to govern with fairness, earned him the respect of his people and even his enemies.

Modern leaders can learn from Salah ad-Din's example by prioritizing fairness in their leadership, treating others with respect, and ensuring that justice is a core value in all aspects of their decision-making. By leading with fairness and justice, today's leaders can build lasting legacies of trust, loyalty, and success.

Lesson for Today: Justice as the Cornerstone of Trust in Leadership

JUSTICE IS THE BEDROCK upon which trust is built in leadership. When leaders act with fairness, their followers develop a deep sense of trust and respect, leading to long-term loyalty and a unified effort toward shared goals. Salah ad-Din's legacy as a ruler who prioritized justice above personal gain or revenge serves as a timeless lesson for leaders today. This chapter explores how creating systems and making decisions that are just and balanced can foster trust and loyalty in any organization or team, ensuring sustainable success.

1. Justice as the Foundation of Trust

HISTORICAL INSIGHT: Salah ad-Din's commitment to justice was the foundation of his leadership. His fair treatment of all subjects, regardless of religion or status, established him as a ruler whose authority was rooted in ethical principles, not just military power. This sense of justice allowed him to build a loyal and stable society, where even those who had once been his enemies came to respect him.

Modern Application: In today's world, leaders who prioritize justice in their decision-making earn the trust of their teams and stakeholders. Justice means treating everyone fairly, applying rules consistently, and making decisions that are free from bias or favoritism. When followers see that their leader is just, they are more likely to trust their judgment, support their decisions, and remain loyal in the long term.

- **Example**: A company leader who applies the same standards and expectations to all employees, regardless of their position or personal relationship, fosters an environment of trust. Employees feel confident that their efforts will be recognized fairly, leading to greater motivation and loyalty.

Building Trust Through Consistency: Justice requires consistency in leadership. Leaders who make just and fair decisions, even when it's difficult, build trust over time. Consistency in applying justice ensures that followers believe in the leader's integrity and are more likely to stay loyal, even in challenging situations.

- **Example**: A manager who consistently applies the company's policies on promotions and rewards based on merit rather than personal favoritism ensures that employees believe in the fairness of the system. This consistency strengthens their trust in the leadership, even when they themselves are not directly benefiting.

---

2. Making Balanced and Fair Decisions

HISTORICAL INSIGHT: Salah ad-Din's decisions, both in governance and warfare, were often characterized by balance and fairness. Whether he was negotiating terms of surrender with defeated Crusaders or resolving disputes between different communities, he always sought to find a just solution that respected all parties involved. His ability to make fair decisions earned him the loyalty of his subjects and the respect of his enemies.

Modern Application: Leaders today must strive to make balanced and fair decisions in every situation. This means listening to all perspectives, considering the long-term impact of decisions, and ensuring that outcomes are equitable. Fair decision-making builds credibility and prevents resentment, as people feel that their voices have been heard and respected, even if the final decision does not fully align with their wishes.

- **Example**: In a business setting, a leader who is faced with budget cuts might choose to involve team members in discussions about how resources should be allocated. By considering input from different departments and making a decision that balances the needs of the organization with the well-being of employees, the leader ensures that the process is perceived as fair.

Avoiding Bias and Favoritism: Justice requires leaders to actively avoid bias and favoritism in their decision-making. This means being aware of personal preferences or unconscious biases that might affect judgments and ensuring that decisions are made based on objective criteria. Leaders who focus on fairness rather than favoritism build stronger, more unified teams.

- **Example**: A school principal faced with a disciplinary issue involving two students from different backgrounds should ensure that the same rules and standards are applied equally to both, regardless of external pressures or personal biases. By doing so, the principal fosters a sense of fairness and equality in the school community.

---

3. Creating Systems that Promote Fairness and Justice

HISTORICAL INSIGHT: Salah ad-Din's governance was rooted in creating systems of justice that applied to all his subjects. He appointed local leaders who were known for their fairness and ensured that the legal systems in his territories upheld the principles of justice. This system of governance allowed him to maintain stability and loyalty across a diverse and multi-religious empire.

Modern Application: Leaders today can create systems within their organizations or teams that promote fairness and justice. This might involve setting up transparent processes for promotions, implementing equitable policies for conflict resolution, or ensuring that everyone has equal access to opportunities. Systems that are designed to be fair and just build trust and prevent issues of favoritism or bias from undermining morale.

- **Example**: A company that creates a transparent performance review system, where employees are evaluated based on clear, measurable criteria, ensures that promotions and rewards are distributed fairly. This kind of system reduces the perception of bias and helps employees feel that their hard work will be recognized.

Ensuring Accountability: Justice in leadership also means holding everyone, including the leader themselves, accountable to the same standards. Leaders who create systems that promote accountability ensure that no one is above the rules, which strengthens the perception of fairness within the organization.

- **Example**: A leader who implements a policy where all employees, including management, must adhere to the same code of conduct fosters a culture of accountability. When employees see that the leadership holds itself to the same standards as everyone else, they are more likely to respect and follow those rules.

---

4. Fostering Long-Term Loyalty Through Just Leadership

HISTORICAL INSIGHT: Salah ad-Din's just leadership earned him long-term loyalty, both from his subjects and from his military followers. His fair treatment of all people, regardless of religion or status, created a deep sense of loyalty and trust that endured through difficult times. Even those who had once fought against him came to respect him because of his unwavering commitment to justice.

Modern Application: Leaders who prioritize justice and fairness are more likely to foster long-term loyalty from their teams. When people feel that they are treated fairly and that their leader values justice, they are more likely to stay committed, even during challenging times. This loyalty becomes a key asset, helping leaders navigate crises and maintain unity within their teams or organizations.

- **Example**: A manager who consistently defends their team's best interests and advocates for fair treatment within the company is more likely to build a team that remains loyal, even during times of restructuring or uncertainty. Team members will stand by a leader who they know treats them with fairness and respect.

Building a Culture of Fairness: Just leadership is about more than individual decisions—it's about creating a culture where fairness and justice are ingrained in the organization's values. Leaders who foster this kind of culture create an environment where loyalty and respect naturally grow, as people feel safe, valued, and respected in their roles.

- **Example**: A company that includes fairness and justice as core values in its mission statement and actively works to implement those values in its policies and practices builds a strong culture of trust. Employees are more likely to remain loyal and motivated when they see that the organization consistently upholds these values.

5. The Long-Term Benefits of Leading with Justice

HISTORICAL INSIGHT: Salah ad-Din's legacy as a just leader has endured for centuries. His focus on fairness, ethical governance, and mercy in warfare earned him a place in history as one of the most respected leaders of his time. The long-term benefits of his just leadership were evident not only in his lifetime but in how his reputation has been remembered and admired by future generations.

Modern Application: Just leadership offers long-term benefits in any context. Leaders who build trust through fairness and justice create stable, loyal teams that are better able to withstand challenges and adapt to change. In the long run, these leaders are more likely to leave behind a positive legacy and achieve sustainable success.

- **Example**: A company led by a CEO who consistently prioritizes ethical practices and fair treatment of employees, customers, and stakeholders is more likely to enjoy long-term success. Not only does this approach build a strong brand reputation, but it also attracts and retains top talent, ensuring continued growth.

Justice as a Legacy: Leaders who make justice the cornerstone of their leadership leave behind a lasting legacy. People remember leaders who were fair and just, and their influence often extends far beyond their immediate circle. By leading with justice, today's leaders can build a legacy that endures through time and inspires future generations.

- **Example**: A political leader who fights for social justice and equality, even when it's unpopular, is likely to be remembered and respected for their principled stance long after their time in office. Their legacy serves as an example of ethical leadership for others to follow.

Conclusion: Leading with Justice for Lasting Trust and Loyalty

SALAH AD-DIN'S LEADERSHIP was built on a foundation of justice, fairness, and respect for all people, regardless of their background or beliefs. His legacy teaches us that justice is the cornerstone of trust in leadership. Leaders who consistently make fair decisions, create systems of accountability, and treat their followers with respect foster long-term loyalty and build organizations that thrive in the face of challenges.

Modern leaders can follow in Salah ad-Din's footsteps by prioritizing justice in their leadership. Whether in business, politics, or personal life, just leadership creates the conditions for lasting success, trust, and respect. By making fairness a core value, leaders can inspire others, build strong teams, and leave behind a legacy of integrity and ethical leadership.

Chapter 8: Leading with Faith

Historical Insight: Salah ad-Din's Faith as a Guide to Leadership

Salah ad-Din was not only a military commander and political leader but also a devout Muslim whose faith deeply influenced his decisions and actions. His adherence to Islamic principles of justice, mercy, and compassion guided his approach to leadership and governance. It was his faith that allowed him to navigate the complexities of war and diplomacy while maintaining a moral compass that inspired both his followers and even his enemies. Salah ad-Din's deep spiritual conviction made him a figure of moral authority, helping to unite the Muslim world and strengthening his legitimacy as a leader.

1. Faith as the Foundation of Moral Authority

HISTORICAL INSIGHT: Salah ad-Din's faith was not just a personal belief system but a driving force behind many of his decisions. His deep devotion to Islam and its values of justice, mercy, and ethical conduct were reflected in the way he ruled, fought, and treated others. His actions were often seen as an extension of his spiritual beliefs, giving him moral authority in the eyes of his followers. Salah ad-Din's religious devotion helped elevate him from being merely a military leader to a spiritual figure who embodied the values of his faith.

Modern Application: In leadership, having a strong foundation of values or beliefs—whether rooted in faith or personal ethics—can provide moral authority that inspires trust and respect. Leaders who are guided by a clear set of principles, rather than purely by ambition or power, are more likely to earn the loyalty of their teams. When decisions are made in alignment with deeply held values, they gain legitimacy, as followers can see that the leader is acting from a place of integrity.

- **Example**: A CEO who leads a company with a commitment to social responsibility, driven by personal values or faith, inspires employees to believe in the mission of the organization. By making decisions that reflect ethical priorities, the leader becomes a figure of moral authority, uniting the team around shared principles.

Moral Authority Through Consistency: Just as Salah ad-Din consistently upheld his values in both governance and warfare, leaders today must demonstrate consistency in their beliefs and actions. Consistency in moral leadership ensures that followers trust their leader's vision, knowing that decisions are guided by values rather than convenience.

- **Example**: A political leader who consistently advocates for human rights, even when it is politically challenging, builds moral authority through their unwavering commitment to justice. This consistent stand for what is right earns them respect from both allies and adversaries.

---

2. Inspiring Devotion Through Ethical Leadership

HISTORICAL INSIGHT: Salah ad-Din's faith-driven approach to leadership earned him deep respect and devotion from his followers. He was not only revered for his military prowess but also for his spiritual leadership. His commitment to fairness, justice, and ethical governance, all grounded in his faith, helped him unify the Muslim world, including factions that had once been divided. His personal example of piety and devotion inspired those around him to follow him not just as a military leader but as a moral guide.

Modern Application: In today's world, leaders who lead with ethical principles, rooted in faith or a strong moral code, inspire deeper loyalty and devotion from their teams. When leaders make decisions that prioritize ethical considerations, they create a culture of trust and respect. Followers are more likely to support a leader they believe is acting in accordance with higher values, rather than simply seeking personal gain.

- **Example**: A manager who consistently acts with integrity, treating their team with respect and fairness, fosters a work environment where employees feel valued. This ethical leadership builds loyalty and inspires employees to go above and beyond in their roles because they believe in the leader's vision.

Faith as a Unifying Force: Just as Salah ad-Din's faith helped unite various Muslim factions, leaders today can use their deeply held beliefs—whether religious or ethical—as a unifying force. When followers see that a leader's values are authentic and aligned with the broader mission, it can create a strong sense of unity and purpose within a team or organization.

- **Example**: A nonprofit leader who is motivated by a strong ethical commitment to environmental sustainability can unite their team and donors around a shared mission. By staying true to their values, the leader inspires others to contribute to the cause with the same level of passion and dedication.

3. Balancing Faith and Practical Leadership

HISTORICAL INSIGHT: While Salah ad-Din's faith was central to his identity, he also balanced his religious convictions with the practical demands of leadership. His decisions were not dogmatic but were guided by a nuanced understanding of justice, mercy, and the realities of governance and warfare. For example, his negotiations with Christian leaders and his fair treatment of prisoners demonstrated that his faith guided him toward mercy, even in times of conflict. He understood that applying faith in leadership required both adherence to principles and flexibility in their application.

Modern Application: Leaders today can take inspiration from Salah ad-Din's ability to balance faith or personal values with practical leadership. It is essential for leaders to stay true to their principles while recognizing the complexities of the situations they face. Leadership that is grounded in values but flexible enough to adapt to real-world challenges ensures that decisions are both ethical and effective.

- **Example**: A business leader who values transparency might face situations where full disclosure could harm the company's competitive advantage. Instead of compromising their commitment to honesty, the leader might find a balanced solution, providing transparency to key stakeholders while protecting sensitive information. This balance allows the leader to stay true to their values while meeting the practical needs of the business.

Flexibility in Applying Values: Salah ad-Din's approach to leadership shows that values do not have to be rigid. Instead, they can be guiding principles that help leaders make the best decisions in a variety of circumstances. Leaders who remain grounded in their values but flexible in their application are better equipped to handle the complexities of modern leadership.

- **Example**: A community leader who values inclusivity might face challenges in accommodating different groups with conflicting needs. By finding ways to balance the needs of each group while staying true to the principle of inclusivity, the leader can maintain their moral authority while effectively managing the situation.

4. Leading with Compassion and Mercy

HISTORICAL INSIGHT: Salah ad-Din's faith encouraged him to lead with compassion and mercy, even toward his enemies. His treatment of prisoners during the Crusades, including his decision to ransom Christian knights rather than execute them, was guided by Islamic principles of mercy and justice. Salah ad-Din's ability to show compassion in the midst of conflict not only reinforced his moral authority but also set him apart as a leader of great ethical stature.

Modern Application: Compassionate leadership is essential in today's world, where conflicts—whether in business, politics, or communities—are inevitable. Leaders who can balance strength with compassion are more likely to earn the respect of their teams and foster long-term loyalty. Compassionate decisions, especially in difficult situations, demonstrate that the leader values the well-being of others and is committed to acting with integrity.

- **Example**: A business leader who chooses to support employees facing personal challenges, offering flexible work arrangements or mental health resources, demonstrates compassion in leadership. This approach not only strengthens employee morale but also builds loyalty and trust within the organization.

Mercy as a Strength: Just as Salah ad-Din's mercy was seen as a form of strength rather than weakness, leaders today can view compassion as a powerful leadership tool. By showing mercy when appropriate—such as forgiving mistakes or offering second chances—leaders demonstrate that they are committed to the long-term success and well-being of their teams.

- **Example**: A manager who forgives an employee's mistake and provides guidance on how to improve, rather than resorting to punitive measures, demonstrates mercy. This act of compassion can motivate the employee to work harder and improve, leading to better long-term outcomes for both the individual and the team.

---

5. Faith as a Source of Resilience

HISTORICAL INSIGHT: Salah ad-Din's faith provided him with a source of resilience, particularly during difficult periods of his leadership. His spiritual beliefs gave him the strength to persevere through the hardships of war, political challenges, and personal losses. By turning to his faith, Salah ad-Din found the inner strength needed to remain calm and focused, even in the most trying circumstances. His resilience, grounded in his faith, inspired his followers to stay committed to his cause, even in the face of adversity.

Modern Application: Leaders today can draw strength and resilience from their faith or personal values, particularly when facing challenges. A strong belief system provides a sense of purpose and direction, allowing leaders to stay focused on their goals even when difficulties arise. By demonstrating resilience, leaders inspire confidence and stability in their teams, helping them navigate tough situations together.

- **Example**: A nonprofit leader facing financial challenges might turn to their core belief in the organization's mission to stay focused and motivated. By remaining resilient and committed to the cause, the leader inspires the team to keep pushing forward, even during tough times.

Faith as a Guiding Light in Crisis: In times of crisis, faith or deeply held values can serve as a guide for decision-making. Leaders who rely on their moral compass to navigate challenges are more likely to make decisions that align with their long-term vision and ethical principles, even when the path forward is uncertain.

- **Example**: A political leader who faces a public health crisis might be guided by their belief in the sanctity of human life, making decisions that prioritize the well-being of the population, even if it means making unpopular or difficult choices.

Conclusion: Leading with Faith and Moral Authority

SALAH AD-DIN'S LEADERSHIP was defined by his deep faith, which guided his decisions and actions as both a military commander and a ruler. His ability to inspire devotion and moral authority through his ethical conduct, compassion, and resilience left a lasting legacy. Salah ad-Din's faith-driven approach serves as a powerful example for modern leaders, showing that leadership grounded in values can inspire loyalty, unite people, and achieve great success.

Leaders today can learn from Salah ad-Din's example by allowing their faith or personal values to guide their actions, balancing ethical principles with practical leadership, and leading with compassion and mercy. By staying true to their moral compass, leaders can build trust, foster unity, and leave behind a legacy of integrity and moral leadership.

Lesson for Today: The Power of Moral or Ethical Grounding in Leadership

WHETHER ONE'S VALUES are drawn from religious faith or a personal sense of ethics, having a strong moral grounding is essential for effective leadership. Leaders with a clear set of principles are better equipped to make decisions that inspire trust, loyalty, and respect. Salah ad-Din's leadership, deeply rooted in his Islamic faith, demonstrates the power of leading with a moral compass that guides not only strategic decisions but also day-to-day actions. This chapter explores how leaders can cultivate and lead with a clear vision based on strong moral values, helping them navigate challenges with integrity and confidence.

1. Defining Your Moral Compass

HISTORICAL INSIGHT: Salah ad-Din's leadership was shaped by his unwavering adherence to the principles of Islam. His faith provided him with a clear moral compass, guiding his decisions and actions. This sense of purpose allowed him to lead with integrity and gave him the strength to balance mercy with justice, even in times of conflict. His actions were consistently aligned with his beliefs, and this authenticity helped him build trust and respect both within his ranks and among his enemies.

Modern Application: Leaders today need a clearly defined moral compass to guide their decision-making processes. Whether grounded in personal beliefs, ethical values, or religious faith, having a strong sense of right and wrong ensures that decisions are principled and align with the leader's core values. This authenticity creates a foundation of trust with team members, clients, and stakeholders, as they can see that the leader's actions are consistent with their stated principles.

- **Example**: A company founder who values sustainability might build their business around eco-friendly practices, even if it means higher costs in the short term. By making decisions that reflect their commitment to sustainability, they build a brand that customers and employees can trust.

Staying True to Core Values: A clear moral compass helps leaders stay grounded in their principles, especially when faced with pressure to compromise. Leaders who remain consistent in their values are more likely to inspire loyalty, as people are drawn to those who act with integrity and stand firm in their convictions.

- **Example**: A political leader who values transparency might face pressure to conceal information in a crisis. By staying true to their commitment to openness, the leader builds credibility with the public, even in difficult situations.

---

2. Making Principled Decisions in Leadership

HISTORICAL INSIGHT: Salah ad-Din's decisions—whether in war, governance, or diplomacy—were guided by his commitment to justice and fairness. His moral principles often led him to show mercy, even to enemies, and to seek peaceful solutions where possible. By making decisions that reflected his ethical beliefs, he earned the respect of both his followers and his adversaries, creating a legacy of principled leadership that has endured through the centuries.

Modern Application: Leaders who make decisions based on a strong sense of ethics inspire confidence and loyalty. Rather than reacting impulsively or making choices based on short-term gains, principled leaders take the time to weigh the moral implications of their decisions. This thoughtful approach not only builds trust but also ensures that the leader's vision remains aligned with their long-term values and goals.

- **Example**: A CEO deciding whether to lay off employees to cut costs might prioritize finding alternative solutions that protect jobs, such as reducing executive salaries or offering voluntary early retirement packages. By making decisions rooted in fairness and compassion, the leader demonstrates that they value the well-being of their employees as much as the bottom line.

Balancing Ethics with Practicality: While staying true to moral principles is essential, leaders must also balance their values with the practical realities they face. Leaders like Salah ad-Din, who managed to balance ethical governance with the demands of warfare and diplomacy, show that it is possible to make principled decisions while still addressing practical needs.

- **Example**: A nonprofit leader who is committed to providing free services to underserved communities might need to find creative ways to generate revenue to sustain the organization. By balancing ethical priorities with practical needs, the leader ensures that the mission remains intact while securing long-term viability.

---

3. Cultivating a Vision Rooted in Moral Values

HISTORICAL INSIGHT: Salah ad-Din's leadership was driven by a clear vision to unite the Muslim world and uphold Islamic principles of justice, mercy, and compassion. This vision, deeply rooted in his faith, allowed him to inspire his followers and give them a sense of purpose beyond military conquest. His leadership was not just about achieving territorial gains but about creating a just and ethical society.

Modern Application: Leaders who cultivate a vision based on strong moral or ethical values can inspire and unite their teams around a common purpose. A clear and principled vision helps align decision-making and provides direction during times of uncertainty or conflict. Leaders who communicate their values-driven vision effectively create a culture where team members feel motivated to contribute toward a shared goal.

- **Example**: A leader in the tech industry who is passionate about data privacy might create a vision for the company focused on developing products that prioritize user security and transparency. By making this vision a core part of the company's identity, the leader inspires employees and customers who share those values.

Inspiring Commitment Through Vision: A vision that is rooted in moral values resonates deeply with people and inspires long-term commitment. When team members believe in the ethical foundation of a leader's vision, they are more likely to stay loyal, even when faced with challenges or setbacks.

- **Example**: A school principal who prioritizes equity in education might develop a vision that ensures every student, regardless of background, has access to the resources they need to succeed. This vision can inspire teachers, staff, and the community to rally behind the cause and work together toward creating a more just and equitable educational environment.

4. Navigating Challenges with Integrity

HISTORICAL INSIGHT: Salah ad-Din faced numerous challenges throughout his reign, from political rivalries to intense military conflicts. Yet, his faith and moral grounding helped him navigate these difficulties with integrity. Whether negotiating peace or making decisions in the heat of battle, he consistently applied his ethical principles, earning him a reputation as a fair and honorable leader.

Modern Application: Leaders today face a wide array of challenges, from economic crises to interpersonal conflicts within their teams. A strong sense of moral or ethical grounding can help leaders navigate these challenges with integrity, ensuring that their decisions align with their values. Leaders who act with integrity, even under pressure, build trust and inspire others to follow their example.

- **Example**: A business leader who faces public backlash over a controversial decision might choose to engage in open dialogue with critics, listen to their concerns, and make adjustments where appropriate. By approaching the situation with transparency and accountability, the leader demonstrates integrity and commitment to ethical decision-making.

Building Trust Through Integrity: Integrity is one of the most important qualities in leadership. When leaders act with integrity—staying true to their principles even when it's difficult—they earn the trust and respect of their teams. This trust is vital for maintaining strong relationships and ensuring that teams remain united during tough times.

- **Example**: A government official who admits to a mistake, takes responsibility, and works to correct the error demonstrates integrity. This honesty helps to rebuild public trust and shows that the leader is accountable to the people they serve.

---

5. The Long-Term Benefits of Leading with Moral Values

HISTORICAL INSIGHT: Salah ad-Din's legacy is remembered not just for his military victories but for his commitment to justice, mercy, and ethical leadership. His deep faith and moral grounding earned him the respect of his followers, his allies, and even his enemies. The long-term impact of his leadership demonstrates the enduring power of principled decision-making and the lasting legacy that comes from leading with integrity.

Modern Application: Leading with strong moral or ethical values has long-term benefits, both for the leader and for the organization or community they lead. Leaders who act with integrity and make principled decisions build a legacy of trust, respect, and loyalty that endures beyond their tenure. This approach creates a stable foundation for long-term success, as teams and organizations are more likely to thrive when guided by ethical leadership.

- **Example**: A CEO who consistently leads with fairness and transparency builds a positive company culture that attracts and retains top talent. Over time, this ethical approach leads to a stronger brand reputation, customer loyalty, and long-term growth.

Leaving a Legacy of Integrity: Leaders who prioritize moral values in their decision-making leave behind a legacy that is remembered for its impact on people and society. By staying true to their principles, leaders can influence future generations and inspire others to lead with integrity.

- **Example**: A civil rights leader who champions justice and equality, even in the face of personal sacrifice, leaves a legacy that inspires future leaders to continue fighting for social change and fairness.

Conclusion: Leading with a Clear Vision Rooted in Moral Values

SALAH AD-DIN'S LEADERSHIP, shaped by his deep faith and commitment to ethical principles, provides a powerful model for modern leaders. His ability to make principled decisions, stay true to his values, and inspire devotion through a clear moral vision shows that leadership grounded in strong ethics has a lasting impact.

Today's leaders can draw from this example by cultivating a clear vision based on moral values, making principled decisions, and navigating challenges with integrity. By leading with a strong sense of ethics, leaders create a culture of trust and loyalty, inspire their teams, and leave behind a legacy of positive, lasting change.

Chapter 9: Loyalty and Trust in Leadership

Historical Insight: Salah ad-Din's Loyalty and the Trust He Built with His Generals and Soldiers

Salah ad-Din's leadership was characterized by an exceptional level of loyalty and mutual trust between himself and his generals, soldiers, and allies. His ability to inspire and maintain the unwavering loyalty of those around him was not merely a product of his military prowess but was rooted in his own deep sense of loyalty, fairness, and respect for his allies and followers. Salah ad-Din's commitment to his people, along with his strategic brilliance, created a culture of loyalty that was crucial to his success. His soldiers followed him not out of fear, but out of genuine respect and admiration, knowing that their leader was equally loyal to them.

1. Earning Loyalty Through Trust and Respect

HISTORICAL INSIGHT: Salah ad-Din's relationship with his generals and soldiers was built on mutual trust and respect. He treated his men fairly, shared in their hardships, and valued their contributions, which fostered deep loyalty. His soldiers knew that Salah ad-Din was not only a brilliant strategist but also a compassionate leader who genuinely cared for their well-being. This trust was reciprocated, and his men were willing to follow him through the most challenging circumstances because they trusted his leadership and believed in his vision.

Modern Application: In leadership today, earning loyalty begins with building trust and demonstrating respect for team members. Leaders who take the time to understand their team, show appreciation for their contributions, and lead by example are more likely to earn the loyalty of their followers. Trust is built through consistency, fairness, and open communication, and when leaders earn the trust of their teams, they inspire deep loyalty and commitment.

- **Example**: A manager who consistently recognizes and rewards the efforts of their team members creates a culture of trust and loyalty. Employees are more likely to stay committed to a leader who values their contributions and supports their growth.

Mutual Trust in Leadership: Just as Salah ad-Din trusted his generals and soldiers to carry out their duties, leaders today must show trust in their teams. Micromanaging or second-guessing team members undermines their confidence and can erode loyalty. By trusting their team to do their jobs, leaders foster a sense of responsibility and empowerment, which strengthens the bond of loyalty.

- **Example**: A project leader who delegates important tasks and trusts their team to execute them independently builds mutual trust. When employees feel trusted, they are more motivated to perform well and remain loyal to the leader.

---

2. Leading by Example and Sharing in Hardships

HISTORICAL INSIGHT: Salah ad-Din was known for leading by example, sharing in the hardships of his soldiers, and living modestly even during times of military success. He did not separate himself from the struggles of his men; instead, he shared their challenges, whether it was enduring the rigors of long campaigns or sacrificing personal comfort for the greater good. This sense of camaraderie and shared experience deepened the loyalty of his followers, who saw their leader as one of them.

Modern Application: Leaders who lead by example and share in the challenges faced by their teams foster a sense of unity and loyalty. When team members see that their leader is willing to work alongside them and endure the same hardships, they feel more connected and motivated to follow that leader's vision. Leading by example also demonstrates that the leader is committed to the team's success, which inspires greater loyalty and respect.

- **Example**: A CEO who works late with their team during a critical deadline or takes on extra tasks during a period of high pressure shows that they are willing to contribute just as much as their employees. This kind of leadership by example builds respect and loyalty within the team.

Shared Struggles Create Stronger Bonds: When leaders experience the same challenges as their team, it strengthens the bond between them. Just as Salah ad-Din's willingness to share in the hardships of his soldiers built deep loyalty, modern leaders who work alongside their teams during difficult times foster stronger relationships and a greater sense of shared purpose.

- **Example**: A non-profit leader who takes part in fieldwork, alongside their staff, during difficult missions demonstrates solidarity and commitment. This shared experience strengthens the bond between the leader and their team, fostering long-term loyalty.

3. Loyalty to Allies and Building Strategic Relationships

HISTORICAL INSIGHT: Salah ad-Din was known for his deep sense of loyalty to his allies. Whether through political alliances or military partnerships, he remained faithful to those who supported him. His loyalty to his allies was not only a moral principle but also a strategic strength, as it helped him maintain strong alliances that were crucial to his military and political success. His ability to cultivate and maintain relationships based on trust and loyalty allowed him to unite disparate Muslim factions and build a cohesive force capable of resisting the Crusaders.

Modern Application: Leaders today must cultivate strong, trust-based relationships with their allies—whether internal or external stakeholders. Loyalty in leadership is about being dependable and standing by your partners in times of need. Leaders who demonstrate loyalty to their allies, clients, or partners build long-term relationships that are vital for success. These relationships are rooted in mutual trust, reliability, and a shared commitment to common goals.

- **Example**: A business leader who remains loyal to their long-term partners during tough economic times, offering support or flexibility, builds a foundation of trust. These loyal partnerships are more likely to endure challenges and lead to future opportunities.

Maintaining Loyalty in Strategic Relationships: Like Salah ad-Din, who maintained strong alliances by being a dependable and loyal partner, modern leaders should prioritize long-term relationships over short-term gains. Loyalty in strategic relationships strengthens alliances and builds a network of support that can be crucial during difficult times.

- **Example**: A leader in a corporate merger who ensures that both parties' interests are protected throughout the process demonstrates loyalty to the partnership. This focus on fairness and mutual benefit ensures that the relationship remains strong, even after the merger is complete.

---

4. The Role of Respect in Fostering Loyalty

HISTORICAL INSIGHT: Salah ad-Din earned the respect of his soldiers and generals through his fair and respectful treatment of them. He valued their input, recognized their contributions, and treated them as partners in his efforts. This mutual respect was a key factor in the unwavering loyalty he received from those who served him. By showing respect to his followers, Salah ad-Din fostered an environment where loyalty was built on mutual admiration and shared goals, rather than fear or coercion.

Modern Application: Leaders who treat their teams with respect foster deeper loyalty and commitment. Respecting the opinions, skills, and contributions of team members creates an environment where people feel valued and motivated to give their best. Respect is earned through consistent, fair treatment and open communication, and when team members feel respected, they are more likely to remain loyal to their leader and the organization.

- **Example**: A manager who listens to their employees' ideas, acknowledges their hard work, and creates a culture of inclusion builds respect and loyalty within the team. Employees are more likely to stay committed to a leader who values their contributions and respects their individuality.

Loyalty Grows from Mutual Respect: Just as Salah ad-Din's respect for his soldiers fostered loyalty, modern leaders who show respect to their teams create a culture of mutual loyalty. Respect is a two-way street, and leaders who demonstrate genuine respect for their team members are more likely to receive it in return, building a strong foundation of trust and loyalty.

- **Example**: A leader who provides constructive feedback, recognizes achievements, and fosters open communication shows respect for their team's growth and development. This respect leads to a more loyal and dedicated workforce.

5. The Long-Term Benefits of Loyalty in Leadership

HISTORICAL INSIGHT: Salah ad-Din's ability to inspire loyalty among his generals, soldiers, and allies played a crucial role in his long-term success. The loyalty he fostered allowed him to maintain stability within his ranks, even in the face of adversity. His loyal followers were willing to stand by him through difficult times, and this sense of unity and commitment helped him achieve his strategic and military goals. The long-term loyalty he inspired became a cornerstone of his leadership legacy.

Modern Application: Loyalty in leadership leads to long-term benefits for both the leader and the organization. Loyal teams are more motivated, more cohesive, and more likely to stick together during challenging times. Leaders who inspire loyalty create a stable, supportive environment where team members are invested in the organization's success. This long-term loyalty not only improves productivity and morale but also strengthens the leader's ability to navigate crises and achieve sustained success.

- **Example**: A company that retains long-term employees who are loyal to the organization is likely to benefit from higher productivity, stronger teamwork, and greater innovation. Employees who are loyal are also more likely to go the extra mile to support the organization's goals.

Loyalty as a Leadership Legacy: Like Salah ad-Din, leaders who prioritize loyalty leave behind a lasting legacy. A leader who fosters deep loyalty within their organization builds a culture of trust, respect, and mutual support that can endure long after they have moved on. This legacy of loyalty becomes a key part of the leader's long-term impact.

- **Example**: A non-profit founder who builds a team of loyal employees and volunteers creates a lasting impact that continues to benefit the organization even after their departure. The loyalty of the team ensures the sustainability and growth of the organization for years to come.

Conclusion: The Power of Loyalty in Leadership

SALAH AD-DIN'S LEADERSHIP was defined by the loyalty he inspired among his generals, soldiers, and allies. His ability to build trust, lead by example, and show deep respect for his followers created a culture of loyalty that was instrumental in his success. His legacy demonstrates that loyalty is not simply commanded but earned through fairness, trust, and mutual respect.

Modern leaders can draw inspiration from Salah ad-Din's example by cultivating loyalty in their own teams and organizations. By leading with trust, sharing in challenges, demonstrating respect, and maintaining loyalty to allies, leaders can create strong, cohesive teams that remain committed through adversity. Loyalty is a powerful force in leadership, and those who prioritize it build a foundation for long-term success and lasting impact.

Lesson for Today: Trust as the Foundation of Success in Leadership

TRUST IS THE CORNERSTONE of any successful team or organization. Without it, even the most talented teams can falter, and the most promising initiatives can fail. Salah ad-Din's leadership was marked by the deep trust he built with his generals, soldiers, and allies, a trust that was forged through transparency, reliability, and genuine care for those he led. Trust is not something that can be commanded; it is earned through consistent actions, honest communication, and a commitment to the well-being of the team. This chapter explores how modern leaders can build and maintain trust to create loyal, cohesive, and high-performing teams.

1. Building Trust Through Transparency

HISTORICAL INSIGHT: Salah ad-Din was known for his honest communication with his generals and soldiers. He was transparent about his intentions and strategies, which helped to foster trust among his followers. His openness ensured that his men knew what to expect from him and could trust that he was acting in their best interest. By being clear about his goals and sharing his vision, he strengthened the bond of trust within his ranks.

Modern Application: In today's world, transparency is one of the most effective ways to build trust within a team or organization. Leaders who communicate openly about their goals, decisions, and challenges create an environment caf trust where team members feel informed and included. Transparency helps to eliminate confusion and fosters a sense of security, as people understand the reasoning behind decisions and feel confident that their leader is acting with integrity.

- **Example**: A manager who regularly updates their team about the company's financial status, upcoming projects, and organizational changes creates a sense of openness. This transparency reassures the team that there are no hidden agendas and that they can trust their leader to keep them informed.

Communicating with Clarity and Honesty: Just as Salah ad-Din's clear communication helped him earn the trust of his soldiers, modern leaders can build trust by being straightforward and honest in their communication. Clear and honest communication builds credibility and prevents misunderstandings, fostering deeper trust between leaders and their teams.

- **Example**: A leader who faces a difficult decision, such as layoffs or restructuring, should communicate the reasons behind the decision clearly and compassionately. By being upfront and transparent, the leader maintains trust, even in challenging circumstances.

---

2. Trust Through Reliability and Consistency

HISTORICAL INSIGHT: Salah ad-Din's reliability as a leader was a key factor in earning the loyalty and trust of his soldiers. He was known for keeping his word, following through on promises, and being consistent in his actions. His generals and soldiers knew they could depend on him to lead them wisely and justly, which created a sense of stability and trust within his ranks. His reliability, even in difficult times, strengthened his leadership and deepened the loyalty of those who served him.

Modern Application: Reliability is a crucial component of trust in leadership. When leaders are consistent in their actions and follow through on their promises, they build a foundation of trust that strengthens their relationship with their team. Leaders who are reliable create a stable environment where team members feel secure in knowing what to expect, which fosters loyalty and long-term commitment.

- **Example**: A project leader who consistently meets deadlines, provides clear guidance, and is dependable in offering support builds trust with their team. Team members are more likely to go above and beyond when they know they can rely on their leader to do the same.

The Power of Follow-Through: Leaders who consistently follow through on their commitments—whether it's delivering on a project or supporting an employee's development—build trust by showing that their word can be trusted. This reliability fosters a culture of accountability and trust within the team.

- **Example**: A department head who promises resources to a team for a major initiative must ensure those resources are provided. By delivering on promises, the leader reinforces trust and shows that they are dependable and committed to the team's success.

---

3. Genuine Care for the Well-Being of Those You Lead

HISTORICAL INSIGHT: Salah ad-Din's deep sense of loyalty to his soldiers and allies was rooted in his genuine care for their well-being. He was known for ensuring that his men were treated fairly, provided for, and protected in times of hardship. This care extended beyond the battlefield—Salah ad-Din made sure his soldiers were well-equipped, had access to medical care, and were fairly compensated. His genuine concern for his followers created a bond of trust that was vital to his success as a leader.

Modern Application: Leaders who show genuine care for the well-being of their teams build trust and loyalty that lasts. When team members feel that their leader is invested in their success and well-being, they are more likely to remain committed and loyal to the organization. Genuine care involves understanding the individual needs of team members, offering support when needed, and fostering an environment where people feel valued and respected.

- **Example**: A manager who takes the time to check in on employees' well-being, offers flexible working arrangements during stressful periods, or provides resources for personal development demonstrates genuine care. This investment in the team's well-being builds trust and strengthens the leader's relationship with their employees.

Creating a Supportive Environment: Leaders who create a supportive and caring environment, where team members feel that their contributions are valued and their well-being is a priority, foster trust. A leader's genuine concern for the personal and professional growth of their team creates a culture of mutual respect and loyalty.

- **Example**: A supervisor who supports an employee through personal challenges, such as offering time off or reduced workloads during family emergencies, builds a sense of trust and appreciation. This level of care creates a loyal and motivated team.

4. Maintaining Trust in Times of Adversity

HISTORICAL INSIGHT: Salah ad-Din's leadership was often tested during times of adversity, such as during the Crusades or when uniting various factions of the Muslim world. Yet, even in the face of these challenges, he maintained the trust of his generals and soldiers by staying true to his principles, being transparent about his decisions, and showing resilience. His ability to maintain trust during difficult times was key to his success in keeping his forces united and motivated.

Modern Application: In leadership, maintaining trust during times of adversity is crucial for long-term success. Leaders who are honest, transparent, and consistent during crises are more likely to retain the trust of their teams. When challenges arise, leaders must communicate openly about the situation, offer reassurance, and demonstrate resilience. Teams that trust their leader during adversity are more likely to remain cohesive and focused on overcoming the challenge.

- **Example**: A company going through financial difficulties might face uncertainty among employees. A leader who communicates openly about the challenges, provides regular updates, and shows commitment to protecting jobs will maintain trust and keep the team united during the crisis.

Staying True to Values in Difficult Times: Leaders who stay true to their values, even in difficult circumstances, reinforce trust with their teams. When leaders demonstrate that they can be relied on to make principled decisions, no matter the pressure, they maintain the trust and loyalty of their followers.

- **Example**: A nonprofit leader who faces funding cuts but remains committed to serving the organization's mission—by finding creative ways to maintain services without compromising core values—demonstrates resilience and maintains trust within the team.

---

5. The Long-Term Impact of Trust on Team Success

HISTORICAL INSIGHT: Salah ad-Din's leadership legacy is built on the loyalty and trust he inspired in his followers. The deep trust he cultivated allowed him to maintain unity and achieve long-term success, even in the face of significant challenges. His ability to build and sustain trust ensured that his generals and soldiers remained committed to him throughout his campaigns, and his leadership continued to be admired long after his time.

Modern Application: Trust is a long-term investment that pays off through team cohesion, loyalty, and sustained success. Leaders who prioritize trust create environments where teams are more motivated, engaged, and committed to achieving shared goals. Trust allows teams to work together more effectively, communicate openly, and overcome challenges with greater resilience.

- **Example**: A leader who consistently builds trust over time will have a team that is more willing to take risks, innovate, and collaborate. Trust creates the foundation for a high-performing team that is capable of achieving long-term success.

Building a Lasting Legacy Through Trust: Like Salah ad-Din, leaders who build trust leave behind a lasting legacy. The impact of trust goes beyond immediate successes—it creates a culture of loyalty and integrity that endures. Teams that are built on trust continue to thrive and succeed, even after the leader has moved on.

- **Example**: A business leader who fosters a culture of trust, transparency, and care within their organization leaves behind a strong, resilient company that continues to perform well, even after their departure.

Conclusion: Trust as the Bedrock of Leadership

SALAH AD-DIN'S LEADERSHIP was built on a foundation of trust—trust earned through transparency, reliability, and genuine care for his people. His legacy shows that trust is not only essential for building loyalty but also for achieving long-term success. Modern leaders can learn from his example by prioritizing trust in their own leadership, creating environments where teams feel valued, supported, and confident in their leader's integrity.

By building trust through open communication, consistency, and genuine care, leaders can create teams that are loyal, cohesive, and capable of overcoming challenges together. Trust is the bedrock of leadership, and those who prioritize it lay the foundation for lasting success and a powerful leadership legacy.

Part IV: Legacy and Reflection

Chapter 10: Leadership Driven by a Higher Purpose

Historical Insight: Salah ad-Din's Ambition for a Greater Cause

Salah ad-Din's ambition was not rooted in personal gain or the pursuit of power for its own sake. Instead, his life's work was dedicated to a cause much greater than himself: reclaiming Jerusalem and restoring unity within the Muslim world. His leadership was driven by his deep commitment to these higher goals, and he remained focused on them throughout his campaigns and governance. Salah ad-Din's selfless dedication to a greater mission earned him the respect and loyalty of his followers, and his legacy endures as an example of purpose-driven leadership.

1. Leading with Purpose Beyond Personal Gain

HISTORICAL INSIGHT: Salah ad-Din's ambition was not about acquiring wealth, expanding personal power, or indulging in luxury. He was deeply motivated by his faith and the desire to reclaim Jerusalem from the Crusaders, viewing this as a sacred duty. His focus on this larger mission allowed him to transcend the usual temptations of power, and he dedicated his resources, energy, and life to achieving this goal. His selflessness and focus on the greater good earned him the admiration of both his allies and his enemies, who respected his commitment to a noble cause.

Modern Application: In today's world, leaders who are driven by a sense of purpose beyond personal advancement inspire deeper loyalty and trust from their teams. When leaders demonstrate that their ambitions are aligned with a greater mission—whether it's social impact, corporate responsibility, or a community-focused goal—people are more likely to rally behind them. Leadership that is focused on creating positive change, rather than personal enrichment, motivates teams to work toward shared goals with passion and dedication.

- **Example**: A nonprofit leader who is driven by a commitment to alleviating poverty or promoting environmental sustainability demonstrates purpose-driven leadership. By focusing on the mission rather than personal accolades, the leader inspires their team to work harder toward achieving the organization's goals.

Focusing on Collective Success: Just as Salah ad-Din focused on the larger goal of reclaiming Jerusalem and uniting the Muslim world, modern leaders can emphasize the collective success of their teams or organizations. When leaders make decisions that prioritize the well-being of the whole group over personal gain, they build trust and inspire greater commitment.

- **Example**: A business leader who prioritizes company-wide success over personal bonuses by reinvesting profits into employee development or community outreach shows that their leadership is driven by collective well-being rather than individual wealth.

2. The Power of a Higher Cause to Inspire Others

HISTORICAL INSIGHT: Salah ad-Din's dedication to reclaiming Jerusalem and uniting the Muslim world was not only a personal mission—it was a rallying cry for thousands of people who joined his cause. His leadership inspired devotion because his followers understood that his ambition was not self-serving but aimed at fulfilling a greater purpose. This higher cause gave his campaigns meaning, helping to unite different factions and mobilize support from across the Muslim world.

Modern Application: Leaders who align their vision with a higher cause—whether it's social justice, environmental protection, or innovation for the betterment of society—are more likely to inspire loyalty and commitment from their teams. A clearly articulated mission that transcends individual gain helps unite people behind a common purpose. When followers believe in the higher cause, they are more likely to be engaged, motivated, and willing to go the extra mile.

- **Example**: A tech entrepreneur who builds a company around the mission of creating technology that improves people's lives, such as developing accessible healthcare solutions, inspires employees to work toward something bigger than just business success. This purpose-driven mission motivates team members to innovate and push boundaries in service of the larger goal.

Uniting People Around a Shared Purpose: Like Salah ad-Din, who brought together diverse groups under a shared mission, modern leaders can foster unity by clearly defining the purpose that drives their leadership. A compelling cause that benefits the greater good can bridge differences and motivate individuals to set aside personal ambitions for the sake of a larger goal.

- **Example**: A community leader who advocates for clean water access in underserved regions unites diverse groups—volunteers, donors, and local governments—under the shared mission of improving public health and quality of life.

---

3. Staying Committed to a Cause in the Face of Challenges

HISTORICAL INSIGHT: Salah ad-Din faced significant challenges in his quest to reclaim Jerusalem and unite the Muslim world, including political rivalries, military defeats, and resource shortages. Despite these obstacles, he remained steadfast in his commitment to his cause, never losing sight of the larger goal. His perseverance and ability to keep his eye on the bigger picture helped him overcome challenges and ultimately succeed in his mission. His resilience in the face of adversity demonstrated his dedication to a purpose greater than himself.

Modern Application: Leaders today often face setbacks and challenges in pursuing their goals, but those who remain committed to a higher purpose are more likely to succeed in the long run. Staying focused on the larger mission, even when things get tough, helps leaders navigate obstacles with resilience. By keeping the team's efforts aligned with the greater goal, leaders can maintain morale and encourage perseverance, even during challenging times.

- **Example**: A social entrepreneur working to address food insecurity might face financial difficulties or bureaucratic hurdles. However, by staying committed to the larger purpose—feeding underserved communities—the leader can inspire their team to keep pushing forward, finding creative solutions to overcome obstacles.

Perseverance as a Key to Success: Just as Salah ad-Din persevered through multiple challenges in his quest for Jerusalem, modern leaders must stay committed to their purpose, even when immediate results are not forthcoming. Leaders who demonstrate resilience in the pursuit of a larger cause inspire their teams to adopt the same mindset, fostering a culture of perseverance and determination.

- **Example**: A company that is developing breakthrough medical treatments might face years of research setbacks and funding challenges. A leader who stays committed to the mission of improving patient outcomes will inspire their team to continue working toward success, despite the obstacles.

---

4. Leading Selflessly for the Benefit of Others

HISTORICAL INSIGHT: Salah ad-Din's leadership was marked by his selflessness and dedication to the greater good. He lived modestly and was known for putting the needs of his people and soldiers above his own comfort. He devoted his life to a cause that he believed would benefit not only himself but future generations of the Muslim world. This selflessness deepened the loyalty of his followers, who respected his willingness to sacrifice personal gains for the larger mission.

Modern Application: Leaders who demonstrate selflessness—putting the needs of their teams, organizations, or causes above their own personal interests—earn deeper respect and loyalty from those they lead. Selfless leadership fosters a culture of mutual support, where team members are more likely to prioritize the success of the collective over individual achievements. By leading with humility and focusing on the greater good, leaders create a lasting impact that extends beyond their own tenure.

- **Example**: A CEO who forgoes personal bonuses to reinvest in employee training and development demonstrates selflessness and commitment to the long-term success of the organization. This approach fosters loyalty and inspires employees to contribute to the company's success.

Creating a Culture of Service: Leaders who model selflessness in their leadership inspire others to do the same. By showing that their decisions are driven by the desire to serve a greater cause, rather than personal gain, leaders create a culture where team members are motivated by purpose rather than competition.

- **Example**: A nonprofit leader who consistently focuses on serving the community—whether through long hours or hands-on involvement in fieldwork—sets the tone for an organization dedicated to service. This culture encourages team members to put the mission first, fostering greater collaboration and dedication.

---

5. Leaving a Legacy Through Purpose-Driven Leadership

HISTORICAL INSIGHT: Salah ad-Din's legacy endures not just because of his military victories but because of the larger purpose that guided his leadership. His dedication to reclaiming Jerusalem and restoring unity within the Muslim world left a lasting impact that extended beyond his lifetime. His selfless leadership, driven by a higher cause, continues to be admired and respected centuries later. Salah ad-Din's life reminds us that leaders who are motivated by a sense of purpose leave behind legacies that endure far longer than personal accolades or material success.

Modern Application: Leaders who are driven by a clear sense of purpose create legacies that last beyond their time in leadership. Purpose-driven leadership inspires future generations and leaves a lasting mark on the organizations, communities, or movements they lead. By focusing on long-term goals that benefit others, rather than short-term personal gains, leaders can build a legacy of meaningful impact that endures.

- **Example**: A political leader who champions education reform, ensuring that future generations have access to quality education, leaves behind a legacy that continues to improve society long after they have left office.

Building a Legacy Around a Higher Purpose: Like Salah ad-Din, modern leaders who dedicate their efforts to a higher cause—whether in business, philanthropy, or public service—leave behind a meaningful legacy. Leaders who prioritize purpose over personal gain create a foundation for lasting impact, influencing those who follow in their footsteps to carry on the mission.

- **Example**: A tech founder who builds a company focused on sustainable energy solutions leaves a legacy of environmental stewardship. Even after stepping down, the founder's vision continues to shape the industry and inspire future leaders to pursue ethical, purpose-driven innovation.

Conclusion: Leading with a Higher Purpose

SALAH AD-DIN'S AMBITION was rooted in a cause far greater than himself, and this dedication to a higher purpose defined his leadership and his legacy. His selflessness, resilience, and commitment to the well-being of others serve as a powerful example of how leaders can transcend personal gain to achieve lasting impact. Modern leaders can draw inspiration from Salah ad-Din's leadership by staying focused on the bigger picture, leading with purpose, and dedicating themselves to a mission that benefits others.

Leaders who align their ambitions with a greater cause inspire loyalty, motivate teams, and leave behind legacies that continue to make a positive difference long after their leadership has ended. Purpose-driven leadership is not only a path to success but also a way to ensure that the leader's impact endures for future generations.

Lesson for Today: The Power of Purpose in Modern Leadership

IN TODAY'S FAST-PACED and often self-centered world, leaders who focus on a cause greater than their own personal success can truly transform their teams, organizations, and even industries. Salah ad-Din's leadership was grounded in a purpose that went far beyond personal ambition; he was driven by a larger vision to reclaim Jerusalem and unite the Muslim world. This focus on a higher mission allowed him to inspire others, rally support, and leave a lasting legacy. Modern leaders, too, can create transformative change by leading with a clear sense of purpose that transcends individual goals and focuses on collective success.

1. Defining a Purpose Beyond Personal Ambition

HISTORICAL INSIGHT: Salah ad-Din's leadership was guided by his unwavering dedication to reclaiming Jerusalem and restoring unity within the Muslim world. His personal ambitions were secondary to this larger purpose, which gave his leadership depth and meaning. His vision was about restoring justice and fulfilling a sacred duty, not just personal power or wealth.

Modern Application: Leaders who define their leadership around a purpose larger than their own personal ambition are more likely to inspire and engage their teams. When a leader's goals are rooted in a larger vision—whether it's improving society, driving innovation, or advancing a cause—followers can see that their work contributes to something meaningful. This sense of shared purpose is a powerful motivator and helps align the team toward achieving long-term success.

- **Example**: A business leader who prioritizes environmental sustainability and ethical practices, rather than focusing solely on profits, inspires employees and customers who share those values. This purpose-driven approach creates a deeper connection to the company's mission.

Creating a Purpose-Driven Vision: Just as Salah ad-Din's leadership was shaped by his broader mission, modern leaders should clearly articulate a purpose that extends beyond personal advancement. This vision can serve as a guiding force for decision-making and inspire others to rally behind a common cause.

- **Example**: A tech entrepreneur focused on closing the digital divide by providing affordable technology access to underserved communities creates a purpose-driven vision that motivates the team to work toward a meaningful goal.

---

2. Inspiring Others with a Vision That Transcends Individual Success

HISTORICAL INSIGHT: Salah ad-Din's purpose-driven leadership united factions and inspired loyalty from those who followed him. His vision of reclaiming Jerusalem and uniting the Muslim world transcended his own personal success, becoming a cause that others were willing to support and sacrifice for. This larger vision gave meaning to his campaigns and motivated his followers to persevere even in the face of great challenges.

Modern Application: Leaders who focus on a collective vision that benefits others—whether it's a community, a team, or society as a whole—are more likely to inspire deep loyalty and commitment from those they lead. When people feel that their efforts contribute to something bigger than individual success, they become more invested in the cause. A shared purpose provides a sense of fulfillment that can drive greater engagement, innovation, and perseverance.

- **Example**: A healthcare executive who is driven by the mission of improving access to medical care in low-income areas can inspire doctors, nurses, and support staff to join the cause. The shared vision of providing care to underserved populations motivates the team to work tirelessly, even in challenging conditions.

Building a Shared Mission: Leaders should clearly communicate how each team member's contributions align with the larger mission. By helping team members see the impact of their work beyond individual achievements, leaders can create a sense of shared ownership and pride in the collective success.

- **Example**: A nonprofit leader focused on educational reform can emphasize how every donation, volunteer hour, and outreach effort contributes to long-term changes in public education systems. This shared mission gives volunteers and employees a sense of ownership and fulfillment in their work.

---

3. Persevering Through Challenges with a Greater Purpose

HISTORICAL INSIGHT: Salah ad-Din's determination to reclaim Jerusalem was tested by numerous challenges, including military setbacks and political rivalries. Yet, his commitment to his higher purpose allowed him to persevere through these obstacles. His resilience was driven by a belief in the larger mission, rather than personal gain, and this gave him the strength to lead effectively even in the most difficult times.

Modern Application: Leadership, especially when focused on a higher purpose, often involves navigating difficult challenges. Leaders who remain committed to their purpose, even when faced with setbacks, inspire confidence and resilience in their teams. A strong sense of purpose helps leaders stay focused on the bigger picture, allowing them to push through adversity and keep the team motivated.

- **Example**: A social entrepreneur focused on solving homelessness might encounter financial difficulties or policy roadblocks. However, by staying focused on the larger mission of creating lasting housing solutions, the leader can inspire their team to persevere, finding innovative ways to overcome obstacles.

Staying Focused on the Long-Term Vision: Like Salah ad-Din, who stayed focused on his goal despite setbacks, modern leaders should keep their long-term vision front and center, using it as a guide during difficult times. This helps teams remain committed, even when immediate success seems elusive.

- **Example**: A company developing renewable energy solutions may face technological challenges, but a leader who continues to emphasize the long-term goal of reducing carbon emissions keeps the team motivated to push forward, knowing their work is contributing to a global cause.

---

4. Fostering a Selfless Approach to Leadership

HISTORICAL INSIGHT: Salah ad-Din's leadership was marked by a selfless dedication to his cause. He lived modestly, shared in the hardships of his soldiers, and focused on the well-being of his people rather than personal luxuries. His selflessness strengthened the loyalty of his followers, who respected him for putting the greater good above his own interests.

Modern Application: In modern leadership, selflessness can be a transformative quality. Leaders who prioritize the needs of their teams, customers, or communities over their own personal gains build deeper trust and loyalty. A selfless approach to leadership fosters a culture of service, where the focus is on collective success rather than individual achievement.

- **Example**: A CEO who sacrifices personal bonuses to ensure that employees are fairly compensated during tough financial times demonstrates a selfless approach. This builds trust and loyalty, as employees see that the leader is genuinely invested in their well-being.

Empowering Teams Through Selflessness: Leaders who focus on empowering their teams rather than seeking recognition for themselves create an environment where everyone can thrive. This kind of leadership encourages collaboration and inspires individuals to contribute to the collective success.

- **Example**: A project manager who consistently gives credit to their team for successes, while taking responsibility for challenges, fosters a culture of empowerment. Team members feel valued and motivated to contribute their best efforts.

---

5. Leaving a Legacy Through Purpose-Driven Leadership

HISTORICAL INSIGHT: Salah ad-Din's leadership left a lasting legacy not only because of his military victories but because of the larger purpose he dedicated his life to. His commitment to a higher cause—reclaiming Jerusalem and uniting the Muslim world—ensured that his impact would be felt for generations. His selflessness, dedication, and vision for the greater good are remembered and admired to this day.

Modern Application: Leaders who align their efforts with a purpose beyond personal ambition create legacies that endure. Purpose-driven leadership influences future generations and leaves a lasting impact on organizations, communities, or movements. By focusing on goals that benefit others, leaders can create positive change that extends beyond their immediate success.

- **Example**: A philanthropist who dedicates their resources to fighting climate change creates a legacy that influences environmental policy and inspires future leaders to continue the fight for sustainability.

Creating Enduring Impact: Leaders who dedicate themselves to a higher cause build legacies that go beyond their tenure. By focusing on lasting, positive change rather than short-term gains, they create a ripple effect that benefits future generations.

- **Example**: A politician who champions equal access to education, ensuring that future generations have opportunities for learning, leaves a legacy that shapes the lives of countless individuals long after their term in office has ended.

Conclusion: Leading with a Purpose That Transcends Individual Success

SALAH AD-DIN'S LEADERSHIP was defined by his dedication to a cause far greater than personal ambition, and his ability to unite people around this higher purpose allowed him to achieve lasting success. His example shows that leaders who focus on a vision that transcends individual success can inspire deep loyalty, persevere through challenges, and create a legacy that endures.

Modern leaders can transform their teams and organizations by defining a clear purpose that benefits others, communicating that vision, and staying committed to it even in the face of adversity. By leading with a sense of purpose beyond personal gain, leaders can inspire others to work toward collective success and leave behind a lasting, positive impact.

Chapter 11: Legacy Through Character and Conduct

Historical Insight: Salah ad-Din's Legacy of Fairness, Justice, and Compassion

Salah ad-Din's legacy was not solely built on his military victories but on the way he conducted himself as a leader and ruler. His reputation for fairness, justice, and compassion earned him admiration not only from his fellow Muslims but also from his Christian adversaries during the Crusades. His treatment of prisoners, his respect for religious sites, and his emphasis on just governance were key factors in shaping his long-term impact. Salah ad-Din's legacy endures because of the character he displayed in leadership, setting a timeless example of how conduct can define a leader's lasting influence.

1. Earning Respect Through Fairness and Justice

HISTORICAL INSIGHT: Salah ad-Din's commitment to justice and fairness was central to his leadership. Whether dealing with his own people or with his enemies, he consistently applied principles of fairness. His treatment of prisoners of war, for example, was merciful and humane compared to the brutal norms of the time. After capturing Jerusalem in 1187, Salah ad-Din spared the lives of the city's Christian inhabitants, allowing them safe passage rather than seeking revenge for the Crusaders' earlier slaughter of Muslims. His fair and just approach earned him respect and admiration even from those who had fought against him.

Modern Application: Leaders who act with fairness and justice, both in their decisions and interactions with others, earn respect and loyalty. A reputation for being fair and just creates a strong foundation of trust, not only with team members but also with partners and competitors. Fairness fosters a positive environment where people feel secure and valued, and where conflicts can be resolved with integrity.

- **Example**: A business leader who ensures that promotion and compensation decisions are based on merit rather than favoritism creates an environment of fairness. Employees trust that their hard work will be recognized and rewarded, which fosters a culture of motivation and loyalty.

Building Trust Through Fairness: Just as Salah ad-Din earned the trust of his people and even his adversaries through his fair conduct, modern leaders can build trust by applying fairness in all their dealings. Fairness ensures that decisions are transparent and free of bias, creating a stable and cohesive team.

- **Example**: A manager who listens to both sides during a workplace conflict and makes decisions based on objective facts, rather than personal relationships, demonstrates fairness. This builds trust within the team and ensures that all members feel respected and heard.

---

2. Leading with Compassion and Humanity

HISTORICAL INSIGHT: Salah ad-Din's leadership was characterized by his deep compassion and humanity. Despite being a powerful military commander, he showed mercy to his enemies and compassion to the vulnerable. His treatment of prisoners during the Crusades—offering them fair terms of release and protecting civilians—was in stark contrast to the brutal practices of many of his contemporaries. His compassionate nature extended to his own people as well, as he worked to ensure that his subjects were treated with dignity and fairness under his rule.

Modern Application: Compassionate leadership is a powerful tool for building strong, loyal teams and creating a positive organizational culture. Leaders who demonstrate empathy and care for the well-being of those they lead foster greater engagement and loyalty. Compassionate leaders create environments where team members feel valued, supported, and motivated to perform their best, knowing that their leader genuinely cares about their well-being.

- **Example**: A leader who supports employees dealing with personal challenges—by offering flexible work arrangements or mental health resources—demonstrates compassion. This type of leadership builds strong bonds of loyalty and creates a more engaged, motivated team.

Balancing Strength with Compassion: Like Salah ad-Din, who balanced his military strength with compassion, modern leaders can show that strength in leadership doesn't exclude empathy. Compassionate leaders inspire others not through fear, but through respect and a shared sense of humanity.

- **Example**: A CEO who takes the time to personally meet with employees affected by layoffs and offers support, such as job placement services or severance packages, demonstrates compassion. This approach helps maintain morale and preserves the company's reputation even during difficult transitions.

3. Building a Lasting Legacy Through Ethical Conduct

HISTORICAL INSIGHT: Salah ad-Din's legacy endures not just because of his victories but because of the ethical way he conducted himself as a leader. His respect for religious sites, particularly during the recapture of Jerusalem, demonstrated his commitment to ethical leadership. He ensured that Christian holy places were preserved and that pilgrims could continue to visit them, showing respect for the religious beliefs of others. His ability to govern with justice, mercy, and respect for all people cemented his legacy as a ruler whose influence was felt far beyond his lifetime.

Modern Application: A leader's legacy is shaped as much by their ethical conduct as by their achievements. Leaders who govern or lead with integrity, fairness, and respect for others leave behind a lasting positive impact. Ethical leadership builds a foundation of trust, credibility, and respect, which continues to influence future generations and shapes the culture of the organization or community.

- **Example**: A political leader who focuses on transparency, anti-corruption efforts, and protecting the rights of all citizens builds a legacy of ethical governance. This legacy can inspire future leaders to uphold similar values and contribute to a fairer, more just society.

Ethical Leadership as a Long-Term Strategy: Just as Salah ad-Din's ethical approach to leadership has been admired for centuries, modern leaders can focus on building an ethical legacy that outlasts their time in power. Ethical leadership fosters long-term trust and respect, ensuring that the leader's influence continues to resonate.

- **Example**: A founder who builds a company around ethical business practices—such as fair labor policies, sustainable sourcing, and environmental responsibility—creates a legacy of integrity. This ethical foundation can attract loyal customers, inspire employees, and influence the broader industry.

4. Earning Admiration from Allies and Adversaries Alike

HISTORICAL INSIGHT: Salah ad-Din's conduct earned him admiration not just from his allies but also from his adversaries. Christian chroniclers, including those who fought against him during the Crusades, wrote about his noble character and honorable conduct. Richard the Lionheart, one of Salah ad-Din's most formidable opponents, reportedly respected him deeply, acknowledging his fairness and chivalry. This ability to earn admiration from both friends and foes alike is a testament to Salah ad-Din's character as a leader.

Modern Application: Leaders who conduct themselves with fairness, respect, and integrity can earn the admiration of even their critics. When leaders remain principled and ethical in their decision-making, they build a reputation that transcends immediate circumstances. This kind of leadership can bridge divides, foster mutual respect, and build a network of allies and supporters who appreciate the leader's values, even if they do not always agree with their actions.

- **Example**: A business leader involved in a competitive industry might earn the respect of their rivals by consistently applying fair and ethical practices in negotiations, contracts, and client dealings. Even in competition, a reputation for fairness can lead to collaboration and mutual respect in the long run.

Winning Respect Through Integrity: Just as Salah ad-Din earned the respect of his adversaries, modern leaders can build a reputation for integrity that transcends differences. Leaders who stick to their principles, treat others with dignity, and act fairly, even in the face of opposition, leave behind a lasting impression that can open doors for future collaboration and reconciliation.

- **Example**: A politician who engages respectfully with opponents, listens to diverse viewpoints, and prioritizes the common good over partisan politics earns respect from across the political spectrum. This approach fosters unity and constructive dialogue, even in contentious environments.

---

5. Leaving a Legacy That Endures

HISTORICAL INSIGHT: Salah ad-Din's legacy as a fair, just, and compassionate ruler has endured for centuries, shaping how he is remembered in both the Muslim and Christian worlds. His reputation for ethical leadership, respect for others, and dedication to justice ensured that his influence extended far beyond his lifetime. Salah ad-Din's legacy remains a powerful example of how leaders can shape the course of history not just through their achievements but through the way they lead.

Modern Application: Leaders who prioritize fairness, compassion, and ethical conduct leave behind a legacy that endures long after their time in leadership has ended. A positive legacy is not just about what is achieved during a leader's tenure but about the lasting impact of their values and conduct. Leaders who consistently act with integrity and respect for others create an enduring influence that inspires future generations to uphold similar principles.

- **Example**: A corporate executive who champions diversity, inclusion, and ethical business practices leaves a legacy that continues to shape the company's culture long after they retire. This legacy fosters a more inclusive and fair environment for future employees and leaders.

Building a Legacy Through Values: Like Salah ad-Din, who is remembered for his character as much as his victories, modern leaders can focus on building a legacy that reflects their core values. By acting with fairness, respect, and compassion, leaders ensure that their influence is felt for generations to come.

- **Example**: A community leader who dedicates their life to social justice, advocating for marginalized groups, leaves behind a legacy that continues to inspire future activists and leaders to fight for equality and fairness.

Conclusion: The Power of Conduct in Shaping a Leader's Legacy

SALAH AD-DIN'S LEGACY was defined not only by his victories but by his conduct as a fair, just, and compassionate leader. His ability to earn admiration from both allies and adversaries alike, his commitment to ethical leadership, and his deep compassion for others ensured that his impact would endure for centuries. Modern leaders can take inspiration from Salah ad-Din's example by prioritizing fairness, compassion, and integrity in their own leadership.

Leaders who focus on ethical conduct and compassionate governance leave behind legacies that transcend personal achievements, shaping the values and culture of the organizations, communities, and societies they lead. By leading with fairness, justice, and humanity, leaders can create a lasting positive impact that endures long after their time in power.

Lesson for Today: Leadership Is Measured by the Legacy of Values and Actions

TRUE LEADERSHIP IS not defined by short-term victories or fleeting achievements, but by the lasting impact of a leader's values, character, and the way they conduct themselves. Salah ad-Din's leadership was not only about military success; it was about how he ruled—with fairness, wisdom, and compassion. His legacy endures because of his ability to balance strength with empathy, and his dedication to justice over personal gain. This chapter will explore how modern leaders can focus on building a legacy that reflects the enduring qualities of honor, wisdom, and compassion, leaving a lasting impact on future generations.

1. Honor: Building a Legacy of Integrity and Respect

HISTORICAL INSIGHT: Salah ad-Din's legacy was shaped by his unwavering sense of honor. His integrity in dealing with both friends and foes earned him respect from all sides. Whether in battle or diplomacy, Salah ad-Din's actions were guided by a deep commitment to fairness and justice. His decision to spare the lives of Jerusalem's Christian inhabitants after its recapture in 1187, for example, was a testament to his sense of honor, even in the face of potential revenge.

Modern Application: A leader's honor is the foundation upon which their legacy is built. Leaders who consistently act with integrity, fairness, and respect earn the trust of those they lead, and this trust forms the basis of a positive, long-lasting impact. Honorable leadership involves making difficult choices with ethics at the forefront, prioritizing doing what's right over personal or short-term gains.

- **Example**: A CEO who refuses to engage in unethical practices, even when pressured by shareholders to increase short-term profits, demonstrates honor. This decision builds long-term trust and secures the company's reputation as one that values integrity.

Building a Legacy of Integrity: Like Salah ad-Din, modern leaders can focus on building a legacy that reflects integrity in all their dealings. Honor in leadership ensures that a leader's decisions are remembered for their fairness and ethical soundness, inspiring future generations to follow in their footsteps.

- **Example**: A community leader who dedicates their career to fighting corruption, consistently advocating for transparency and fairness, leaves a legacy of honor that will inspire future leaders to continue the fight for justice.

---

2. Wisdom: Leaving a Legacy of Sound Judgment and Insight

HISTORICAL INSIGHT: Salah ad-Din's wisdom in leadership was evident in his ability to navigate complex political and military challenges while maintaining unity and justice. His strategic acumen was balanced by his ability to foresee the long-term consequences of his decisions. He carefully balanced the needs of his military campaigns with the broader goal of creating a peaceful and stable region. His ability to make decisions that balanced strength and diplomacy was a hallmark of his leadership.

Modern Application: Wisdom is a critical quality for leaders who wish to leave behind a lasting legacy. Leaders who demonstrate sound judgment, thoughtful decision-making, and insight into the long-term impact of their actions are better able to create sustainable success. Wisdom also involves knowing when to act decisively and when to seek counsel, understanding that thoughtful leadership requires careful consideration of all factors.

- **Example**: A business leader who takes the time to assess the long-term impact of a major decision, such as entering a new market, shows wisdom by weighing both opportunities and risks. This thoughtful approach leads to sustainable success rather than short-term gains.

Cultivating a Legacy of Wise Leadership: Like Salah ad-Din, leaders today can focus on making decisions that reflect wisdom and foresight. A legacy of wisdom is one that endures, as future generations benefit from the sound structures and policies put in place by leaders who valued insight and thoughtful action.

- **Example**: A public servant who advocates for education reform based on extensive research and the long-term needs of society builds a legacy of wisdom. Their efforts improve the lives of future generations by fostering a more educated and capable population.

---

3. Compassion: Creating a Legacy of Empathy and Humanity

HISTORICAL INSIGHT: Salah ad-Din's compassion was one of his most defining traits. His merciful treatment of prisoners, his care for civilians, and his efforts to minimize unnecessary bloodshed set him apart from many of his contemporaries. He understood that true strength in leadership comes not from cruelty or dominance but from the ability to show empathy and care for others, even in times of conflict. His compassion earned him admiration and loyalty from those he ruled and those he fought.

Modern Application: Compassionate leadership is essential for building a legacy that resonates with others. Leaders who show empathy, who listen to the needs and concerns of their teams or communities, and who prioritize the well-being of those they lead create environments of trust and loyalty. Compassion builds stronger, more cohesive teams, and leaders who are remembered for their kindness and humanity leave a lasting impact that goes beyond their immediate successes.

- **Example**: A company leader who prioritizes employee well-being—providing mental health support, fostering work-life balance, and ensuring fair treatment—demonstrates compassion. This approach not only builds loyalty within the company but also leaves a positive legacy that influences corporate culture long after they are gone.

Creating a Legacy of Compassion: Like Salah ad-Din, leaders today can focus on creating a legacy that reflects compassion and humanity. By leading with empathy, modern leaders can create lasting relationships and a positive impact on the lives of those they lead.

- **Example**: A humanitarian leader who dedicates their life to improving the living conditions of refugees creates a legacy of compassion. Their work not only improves lives in the present but also inspires future generations to continue advocating for the vulnerable.

---

4. Long-Term Impact: Shaping a Legacy That Endures

HISTORICAL INSIGHT: Salah ad-Din's legacy has endured for centuries, not just because of his victories but because of the values he embodied—honor, wisdom, and compassion. His influence stretched beyond his time as a ruler, shaping the way both Muslims and Christians viewed leadership, justice, and governance. His actions left a lasting mark on history, demonstrating that true leadership is measured by the values a leader upholds and the impact they leave behind.

Modern Application: Leaders who wish to leave a long-lasting legacy must focus on the values they embody and the impact they want to have on others. A legacy of honor, wisdom, and compassion creates a ripple effect that influences future generations and shapes the culture of an organization or society. By prioritizing these values over short-term successes, leaders can ensure that their influence endures far beyond their time in power.

- **Example**: A nonprofit founder who builds an organization dedicated to social justice, creating programs that provide lasting support for marginalized communities, leaves behind a legacy that continues to change lives long after they are gone.

Focusing on Lasting Values: Like Salah ad-Din, leaders today should focus on leaving a legacy that reflects their core values. A legacy built on principles of fairness, sound judgment, and empathy will resonate with future generations and continue to inspire positive change.

- **Example**: A political leader who prioritizes human rights and builds coalitions that protect civil liberties creates a legacy that ensures future leaders and citizens remain committed to justice and equality.

Conclusion: Leadership Defined by Values and Lasting Impact

SALAH AD-DIN'S LEADERSHIP was defined not just by the victories he achieved but by the values of honor, wisdom, and compassion that guided his actions. His legacy endures because he focused on creating a long-term impact based on these values, inspiring admiration from allies and adversaries alike. Modern leaders can take inspiration from Salah ad-Din by prioritizing values over short-term success and focusing on the legacy they wish to leave behind.

Leaders who act with honor, who lead with wisdom, and who show compassion for those they serve create legacies that endure for generations. By building a legacy based on these timeless values, leaders ensure that their influence continues to shape the world in positive and meaningful ways.

Conclusion: Applying the Conqueror's Code Today

Practical Application: Timeless Leadership Lessons from Salah ad-Din

Salah ad-Din's life offers profound lessons in leadership, integrity, and compassion that continue to inspire modern leaders, professionals, and individuals. His ability to balance strength with humility, ambition with selflessness, and power with compassion has made him a timeless example of what it means to be an ethical and effective leader. By summarizing key lessons from Salah ad-Din's life, we can explore how these principles can be applied to leadership and everyday life today.

1. Lead with Integrity and Fairness

LESSON FROM SALAH AD-Din: Throughout his life, Salah ad-Din demonstrated a commitment to fairness, justice, and ethical behavior. His decisions, whether in governance or battle, were marked by an unwavering sense of integrity. His fair treatment of prisoners, respect for religious sites, and efforts to unite rival factions through diplomacy earned him admiration from both Muslims and Christians.

Modern Application: Leaders today can apply Salah ad-Din's example by acting with integrity in all their dealings, treating others fairly, and making decisions that prioritize ethics over personal gain.

168

Whether in business, politics, or everyday relationships, fairness builds trust and respect, laying the foundation for long-term success.

- **Actionable Step**: Ensure that decision-making processes in your workplace or personal life are transparent and equitable. Treat all individuals with respect and fairness, even in competitive or difficult situations, as fairness fosters loyalty and trust.

2. Stay Focused on a Higher Purpose

LESSON FROM SALAH AD-Din: Salah ad-Din was driven by a cause greater than himself—the reclamation of Jerusalem and the unification of the Muslim world. His ambition was not motivated by personal wealth or power but by a larger vision of justice and peace. This focus on a higher purpose allowed him to inspire others and persevere through challenges.

Modern Application: Leaders and individuals can draw inspiration from this by defining a purpose that goes beyond personal ambition. Whether it's leading a team, running a company, or pursuing a personal goal, having a sense of purpose that benefits others motivates deeper engagement and dedication.

- **Actionable Step**: Reflect on your core values and identify a higher purpose that aligns with your personal or professional goals. Use this purpose as a guiding principle in decision-making and leadership to inspire those around you and create lasting impact.

3. Lead with Compassion and Empathy

LESSON FROM SALAH AD-Din: One of Salah ad-Din's defining traits was his compassion, even in times of conflict. His merciful treatment of prisoners, his care for civilians, and his willingness to show humanity to his enemies set him apart from many other leaders of his time.

Modern Application: In modern leadership, empathy is a crucial component of effective management and relationship-building. Leaders who show compassion and understanding toward their team, clients, or community build stronger, more loyal relationships. Compassion fosters a culture of trust, well-being, and collaboration.

- **Actionable Step**: In leadership or personal interactions, practice active listening and empathy. Prioritize the well-being of others, offer support when needed, and approach conflicts with a mindset of understanding and reconciliation.

4. Cultivate Wisdom and Strategic Thinking

LESSON FROM SALAH AD-Din: Salah ad-Din's wisdom and strategic insight were central to his success. He was not only a brilliant military strategist but also a diplomatic leader who understood the long-term consequences of his actions. His decisions reflected careful consideration, foresight, and balance between strength and diplomacy.

Modern Application: Modern leaders can apply this principle by taking a long-term view in their decision-making. Wisdom involves balancing immediate needs with future outcomes and considering the broader impact of one's choices. Strategic thinking helps leaders navigate challenges effectively while staying focused on their goals.

- **Actionable Step**: Before making significant decisions, pause to assess both the short- and long-term consequences. Consider how your actions will affect others and whether they align with your long-term goals and values. Seek counsel when needed and remain open to diverse perspectives.

5. Lead by Example and Share in Hardships

LESSON FROM SALAH AD-Din: Salah ad-Din was known for leading by example, sharing in the hardships of his soldiers, and demonstrating humility. He didn't distance himself from the struggles of his people but instead participated alongside them, earning their respect and loyalty.

Modern Application: Leadership by example is one of the most powerful ways to inspire trust and dedication. Leaders who demonstrate the values they wish to instill in others—whether through hard work, humility, or resilience—create a culture of mutual respect and responsibility.

- **Actionable Step**: In leadership, avoid asking others to do things you wouldn't do yourself. Be willing to share in challenges, whether it's working late during a tight deadline or taking responsibility for setbacks. By leading from the front, you inspire others to follow.

6. Build a Legacy of Honor, Wisdom, and Compassion

LESSON FROM SALAH AD-Din: Salah ad-Din's long-lasting legacy was not just due to his victories but because of the honorable, wise, and compassionate way he led. His reputation as a just and ethical ruler has made him a respected figure for centuries, remembered for his conduct as much as his accomplishments.

Modern Application: Every leader, professional, or individual has the opportunity to build a legacy based on their values and actions. It's not just about achieving success but about how that success is achieved. A legacy built on principles of honor, wisdom, and compassion leaves a lasting impact that resonates beyond one's immediate circle.

- **Actionable Step**: Consider how you want to be remembered by those you lead or interact with. Focus on embodying the values that reflect the legacy you want to leave behind—whether it's integrity, empathy, or resilience. Make choices that align with these values, ensuring your actions leave a positive mark.

Conclusion: Applying Salah ad-Din's Principles in Modern Life

SALAH AD-DIN'S LIFE offers timeless lessons in leadership and personal conduct, demonstrating how values such as integrity, compassion, wisdom, and purpose can lead to lasting success. Whether you are a leader, professional, or individual navigating personal challenges, these principles can be applied to guide your decisions and actions.

By leading with fairness, focusing on a higher purpose, and showing empathy and strategic insight, you can build strong relationships, inspire loyalty, and create a legacy that endures. True leadership is not about momentary victories but about the lasting impact of one's values and how they shape the world for future generations.

Challenges for the Modern Reader: Embodying Salah ad-Din's Principles in Daily Life

SALAH AD-DIN'S LIFE provides timeless lessons in leadership, integrity, and compassion, but applying these principles in the modern world can be a challenge. The demands of daily life, the pressures of competition, and the complexity of personal and professional relationships may make it difficult to consistently live by these values. However, true leadership and personal fulfillment come from embodying these principles not just in moments of success but in the daily actions that define who we are and how we influence others. Below are some challenges for the modern reader, encouraging the application of these timeless principles in leadership roles, personal relationships, and community involvement.

1. Challenge: Lead with Integrity in Every Decision

PRINCIPLE: Salah ad-Din's leadership was marked by unwavering integrity. Whether in victory or defeat, he consistently acted with fairness and honor, earning the respect of both allies and adversaries.

Modern Application: In today's fast-paced world, the temptation to cut corners, prioritize short-term gains, or compromise on ethics can be strong. However, integrity is the foundation of lasting success and trust. Whether in leadership roles, personal decisions, or professional work, embodying integrity means doing what is right, even when it's difficult or inconvenient.

- **Challenge**: In your next difficult decision, reflect on how you can prioritize integrity over expediency. Whether it's standing up for what's fair in a work conflict, being honest in a challenging conversation, or refusing to take shortcuts in personal or professional goals, choose to act with integrity.

---

2. Challenge: Act with Compassion in Everyday Interactions

PRINCIPLE: Salah ad-Din was known for his compassion, even toward those who opposed him. His ability to balance strength with mercy made him a leader admired for his humanity as much as for his power.

Modern Application: In the modern world, we are often caught up in our own challenges and ambitions, which can make it easy to overlook the needs and emotions of others. Compassionate leadership, however, is rooted in empathy and understanding. Showing care and kindness toward others, even in small ways, strengthens relationships and builds trust.

- **Challenge**: Practice daily acts of compassion, whether it's listening more attentively to a colleague, offering support to someone in need, or showing patience in a stressful situation. Look for opportunities to extend empathy, especially in moments where it may be easier to be indifferent or dismissive.

---

3. Challenge: Stay Committed to a Higher Purpose

PRINCIPLE: Salah ad-Din's life was driven by a higher purpose—reclaiming Jerusalem and restoring unity within the Muslim world. His leadership was defined by this sense of mission, which transcended personal ambition.

Modern Application: In the modern world, it's easy to become consumed by personal ambition or short-term goals. However, focusing on a higher purpose—whether in your career, community involvement, or personal relationships—can bring deeper meaning to your actions and inspire others to follow your lead.

- **Challenge**: Reflect on your higher purpose. Whether it's making a positive impact in your workplace, supporting your community, or being a source of stability and love for your family, define a purpose that goes beyond individual success. Then, take one concrete step this week to align your actions with that purpose, whether it's volunteering, mentoring, or simply making decisions with your greater mission in mind.

---

4. Challenge: Lead by Example, Not by Command

PRINCIPLE: Salah ad-Din's leadership was grounded in leading by example. He shared in the hardships of his soldiers and led with humility, earning their trust and loyalty through his actions rather than through force or command.

Modern Application: Whether in a formal leadership role or not, people naturally look to how we act more than what we say. True leadership, in personal and professional contexts, is about setting an example that others can follow. It's about demonstrating the values you wish to see in others through your own behavior.

- **Challenge**: In your daily life, think of one area where you can lead by example rather than words. If you want your team to be more diligent, show your work ethic. If you want to foster kindness in your relationships, be the first to offer a kind gesture. By modeling the behavior you wish to inspire, you encourage others to follow.

5. Challenge: Practice Wisdom in Decision-Making

PRINCIPLE: Salah ad-Din's leadership was marked by his wisdom in balancing long-term goals with immediate challenges. His decisions were thoughtful and considered, reflecting both strategic insight and a sense of justice.

Modern Application: In modern life, we are often pushed to make quick decisions, sometimes sacrificing long-term success for immediate gratification. Practicing wisdom means taking the time to consider the broader impact of your actions and making decisions that align with both your values and your long-term goals.

- **Challenge**: In the next important decision you face, practice patience and wisdom. Pause to evaluate the long-term consequences of your choice, seek input from others, and ensure that your decision aligns with your personal or professional values. Resist the pressure to rush into decisions, and instead focus on thoughtful, strategic choices.

---

6. Challenge: Build a Legacy of Honor, Wisdom, and Compassion

PRINCIPLE: Salah ad-Din's legacy was shaped not just by his victories but by his conduct as a leader—his honor, wisdom, and compassion. His influence lasted far beyond his lifetime because he focused on the values that mattered most, rather than short-term success.

Modern Application: In our personal and professional lives, we all leave behind a legacy—whether in the form of relationships, the impact we've had on others, or the way we are remembered. Building a legacy isn't about accumulating wealth or accolades; it's about living a life that reflects the values we hold dear and making a lasting positive impact on those around us.

- **Challenge**: Consider the legacy you want to leave behind. Reflect on how you want to be remembered by family, friends, colleagues, and your community. Then, take one actionable step toward building that legacy, whether it's through acts of service, mentorship, fostering stronger relationships, or contributing to a cause you care about.

Conclusion: Embodying Timeless Principles in Modern Life

THE PRINCIPLES THAT guided Salah ad-Din's leadership—integrity, compassion, wisdom, and a commitment to a higher purpose—are just as relevant today as they were in his time. By challenging ourselves to embody these values in our daily actions, whether in leadership roles, personal relationships, or community involvement, we can create a positive and lasting impact in the world around us.

These challenges invite the modern reader to not only learn from Salah ad-Din's life but to actively apply these lessons to their own lives. By doing so, we can all strive to lead with honor, act with compassion, and build legacies that endure far beyond our immediate successes.

Appendix

Additional Resources on Salah ad-Din and Leadership

1. Books

○ *The Crusades Through Arab Eyes* by Amin Maalouf

A comprehensive account of the Crusades from the perspective of the Arab world, providing valuable insights into Salah ad-Din's leadership during this tumultuous period.

○ *The Life of Saladin: From the Works of Imad ad-Din and Baha ad-Din*

A historical account of Salah ad-Din's life, written by two of his closest companions, offering a detailed view of his leadership and character.

○ *Saladin: The Sultan Who Vanquished the Crusaders and Built an Islamic Empire* by John Man

This biography delves into Salah ad-Din's life and explores his leadership style, emphasizing the qualities that made him both a respected leader and a compassionate ruler.

2. Articles

○ *Saladin and the Battle for Jerusalem: The Man Behind the Myth* (History Today)

A well-researched article that explores Salah ad-Din's strategies and his approach to leadership during the Crusades.

○ *Salah ad-Din: Lessons in Leadership* (Harvard Business Review)

A modern interpretation of Salah ad-Din's leadership principles, with applications to business and organizational management.

3. Documentaries and Videos

○ *Saladin and the Crusades* (BBC)

A detailed documentary that covers Salah ad-Din's leadership and his role in the Crusades, with an emphasis on his legacy.

○ *The Sultan and the Saint* (PBS)

A documentary exploring the interaction between Salah ad-Din and Christian leaders, highlighting his ability to balance diplomacy with military prowess.

Leadership and Personal Development Resources

1. Books

○ *Leadership in War: Essential Lessons from Those Who Made History* by Andrew Roberts

This book covers the leadership styles of various historical figures, including Salah ad-Din, offering insights into how they achieved success.

○ *Dare to Lead* by Brené Brown

This book focuses on compassionate and courageous leadership, resonating with many of the principles demonstrated by Salah ad-Din.

2. **Podcasts**

○ *Leadership and Loyalty* with Dov Baron

A podcast that examines how leaders can build strong, loyal teams, using historical examples like Salah ad-Din to illustrate key points.

○ *The Tim Ferriss Show*

Tim Ferriss frequently interviews leaders and experts on how to apply timeless principles of leadership, success, and personal growth.

Quotes from Salah ad-Din

1. *"I warn you against shedding blood, indulging in it, and making a habit of it, for blood never sleeps."*

○ A reflection on the importance of mercy and avoiding unnecessary violence, demonstrating Salah ad-Din's compassion and ethical leadership.

2. *"My hope is that Jerusalem will be an open city for all religions, a place of peace for all people."*

○ This quote encapsulates Salah ad-Din's vision for unity and his respect for people of all faiths, showcasing his commitment to justice and fairness.

3. *"Honor lies in fulfilling a promise, not in vengeance."*

○ A powerful reminder of Salah ad-Din's integrity and commitment to upholding his word, even in the face of adversity.

Exercises for Applying Salah ad-Din's Leadership Principles

1. Reflection Exercise: Identifying Your Higher Purpose

○ Take 15 minutes to reflect on your long-term goals and values. Write down your answers to the following:

▪ What higher purpose drives your decisions?

▪ How does this purpose benefit others or contribute to the greater good?

▪ How can you align your daily actions with this purpose?

2. Empathy Challenge: Practicing Compassionate Leadership

○ For one week, focus on actively listening to those around you—whether at work, home, or in your community. Make it a point to offer support, ask thoughtful questions, and respond with empathy in challenging situations.

3. Legacy-Building Worksheet

○ Use this worksheet to plan the legacy you want to leave behind:

▪ What values are most important to you?

▪ How do you want to be remembered by your family, colleagues, or community?

▪ What actions can you take now to build that legacy?

Glossary

● **Diplomacy**: The practice of managing negotiations and relationships between nations or groups, which Salah ad-Din excelled at, balancing military action with peace negotiations.

● **Mercy**: The compassionate treatment of enemies or adversaries, a defining trait of Salah ad-Din's leadership style.

● **Ethical Leadership**: A leadership style based on the demonstration of moral principles, fairness, and respect for others, embodied by Salah ad-Din in both war and governance.